WE WHO KNEW

The Journal of an Infantry Subaltern during the Great War

The Journal of an Infantry
Subaltern during the Great War

Matthew Cooper
Edited by A.M. Cooper

The Book Guild Ltd
Sussex, England

The Book Guild Ltd
25 High Street,
Lewes, Sussex

First published 1994

Set in Times
Typesetting by Book Setters International Ltd, Salisbury
Printed in Great Britain by
Antony Rowe Ltd
Chippenham, Wiltshire.

A catalogue record for this book is
available from the British Library

ISBN 0 86332 931 4

CONTENTS

PREFACE

This is an account of life in and out of the trenches written by an infantry subaltern who served in France and Flanders in the Great War. It has recently come to light with other family papers after nearly seventy years. The author was Matthew Cooper, my father, who served on the Western Front during those epic and tragic years.

During the war he kept a diary and other records in which he set down incidents and events which made up his daily life. I read them for the first time a year ago and found them compelling. Here was a personal account which conveyed vividly the life led by so many of our countrymen who found themselves in uniform.

I have strolled through fields and villages in which my father had trudged or fought, and I have driven along roads on which he had marched interminably. Between the journal and my journeying I developed an awareness of a soldier's life in those times, an insight which had previously eluded me.

More importantly, I began to understand something more about the prolonged hardship they suffered, the sense of ever-present danger, the monotony, the labour, the moments of anxiety and fear demanding physical and moral courage, the longing for home, moments of disillusionment, the humour, the sadness, but above all, the comradeship and mutual dependence without which they could not have endured. Soldiers throughout the ages have experienced these, but somehow the sheer awfulness of life in the trenches in the First World War has struck a chord of horror and dismay in succeeding generations.

It is not a military history, nor is it concerned with tactics on the battlefield. It is an eye-witness account of day-to-day events written by a junior officer who served in the trenches, whose inborn sense of duty moved him to carry out orders as best he knew how, as did so many of his contemporaries.

The documents were not written with the view to publication and some editing has been necessary. I have attempted to do this without losing the essence or flavour of my father's text.

There is in many cases a choice between the Flemish and French spelling of the names of towns in Flanders and I have selected the one which I believe will be readily recognised by the reader.

I would like to acknowledge the help I received from the Public Records Office at Kew in making available to me trench maps and other documents and my gratitude to the Trustees of the Imperial War Museum, London for permission to reproduce their photographs.

A. M. Cooper
1993

INTRODUCTION

About the Writer

Matthew Cooper was born in 1892 to an English Protestant family living in Dublin. He was the first son of Mark Bloxham Cooper K.C., a practising barrister at the Bar, who had made his way in the legal profession through brain and ambition, holding many posts as Crown Prosecutor, justifying the promise he had shown as a law student. Matthew's father was foremost an orator who shone at criminal trials. He was a man of difficult temperament and did not cultivate those professional friendships so necessary to secure advancement. His business, always meagre, declined in time and he struggled to earn a living. Success did however eventually come and with it eminence and financial security when, at the late age of 64, he was appointed to the Judicial Bench in Dublin by the Lord Lieutenant General.

Matthew's mother, Susannah Lloyd, also came from an English family, well-connected but not affluent. Her brother, Major General Sir Owen Lloyd, KCB, was awarded the V.C. in 1893 when serving in Burma as a Surgeon-Major on the British Army Medical Staff.

Matthew, his elder sister and two brothers were born as the Victorian Age was drawing to its close and brought up in a home atmosphere of intense loyalty to the British Crown. He remembered the soldiers, resplendent in their full dress uniform, colours flying and bands playing, marching proudly to the station on their way to South Africa. At the age of eight he thrilled to see Queen Victoria, bent and bowing in her black bonnet, riding through Dublin in her coach, in acknowledgment of the deeds of the Irish regiments in the Boer War.

He went as a day-boy to Wesley College, a school similar in standard to the grammar school of later years, where, in his own words, he 'drifted, derived little satisfaction and made no real effort to work for a profession or other occupation'. He was 16 when at his father's instigation, he entered the bank at a salary of £40 a year. Two years later he was glad to leave home because of domestic tensions caused by financial anxiety and his somewhat overbearing father whose career was languishing at the time.

During Easter 1910 he was on a visit to a cousin in Tipperary, a curate in a local parish, when he met May Burgess, six years younger than he. They soon became sweethearts, meeting when they could over the next few years. In 1913 he brought her home to meet his mother, his father being away on Circuit.

Matthew was at home with his parents during the fateful August Bank Holiday weekend of 1914 at the outbreak of the Great War.

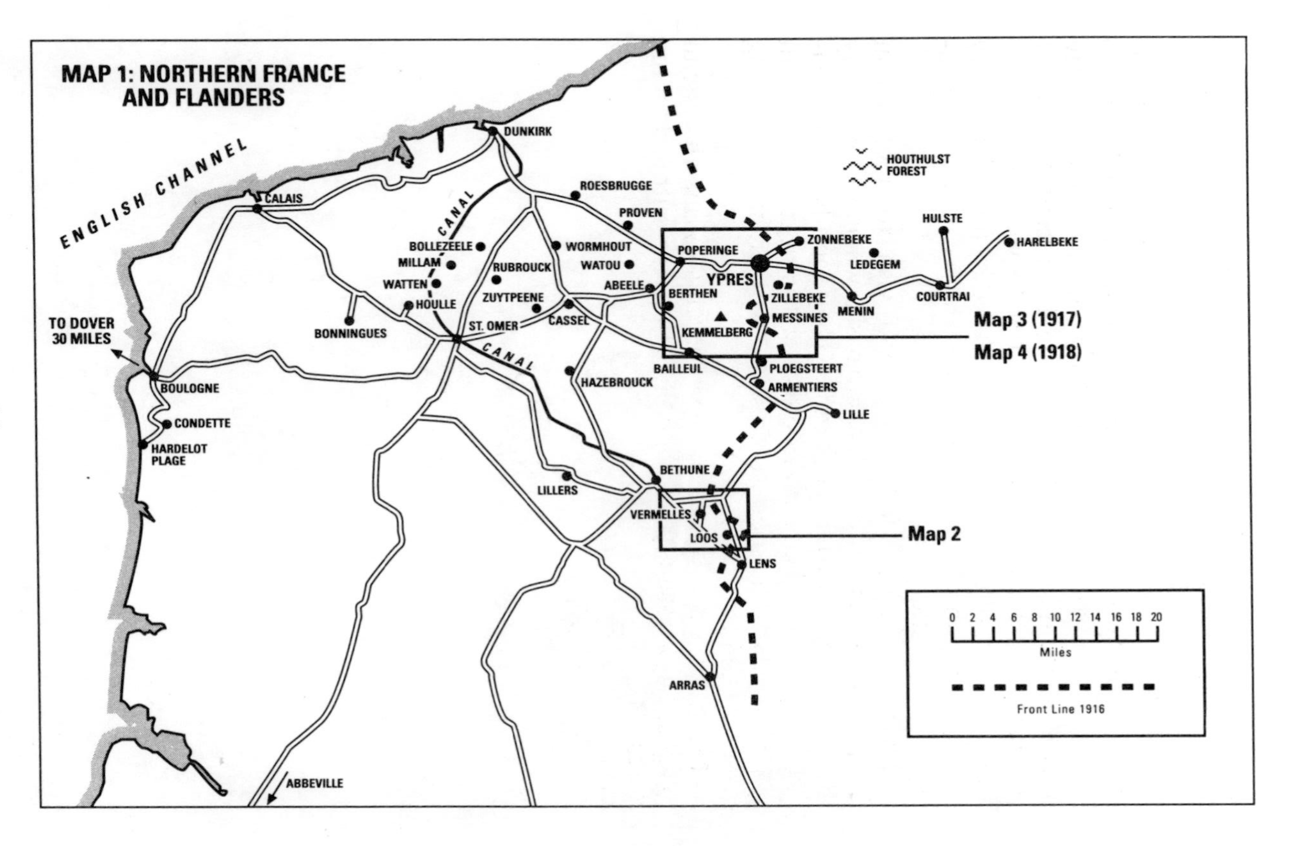
MAP 1: NORTHERN FRANCE AND FLANDERS
ENGLISH CHANNEL
DUNKIRK
CALAIS
CANAL
ROESBRUGGE
PROVEN
HOUTHULST FOREST
HULSTE
HARELBEKE
ZONNEBEKE
LEDEGEM
BOLLEZEELE
MILLAM
WATTEN
HOULLE
RUBROUCK
WORMHOUT
WATOU
POPERINGE
YPRES
ABEELE
BERTHEN
ZILLEBEKE
MENIN
COURTRAI
ZUYTPEENE
CASSEL
MESSINES
KEMMELBERG
TO DOVER 30 MILES
BONNINGUES
ST. OMER
Map 3 (1917)
Map 4 (1918)
CANAL
BAILLEUL
PLOEGSTEERT
HAZEBROUCK
ARMENTIERS
BOULOGNE
LILLE
CONDETTE
HARDELOT PLAGE
BETHUNE
LILLERS
VERMELLES
LOOS
Map 2
LENS
0 2 4 6 8 10 12 14 16 18 20
Miles
Front Line 1916
ARRAS
ABBEVILLE

PART 1 1914-1916

'Something more Profound than Patriotism'

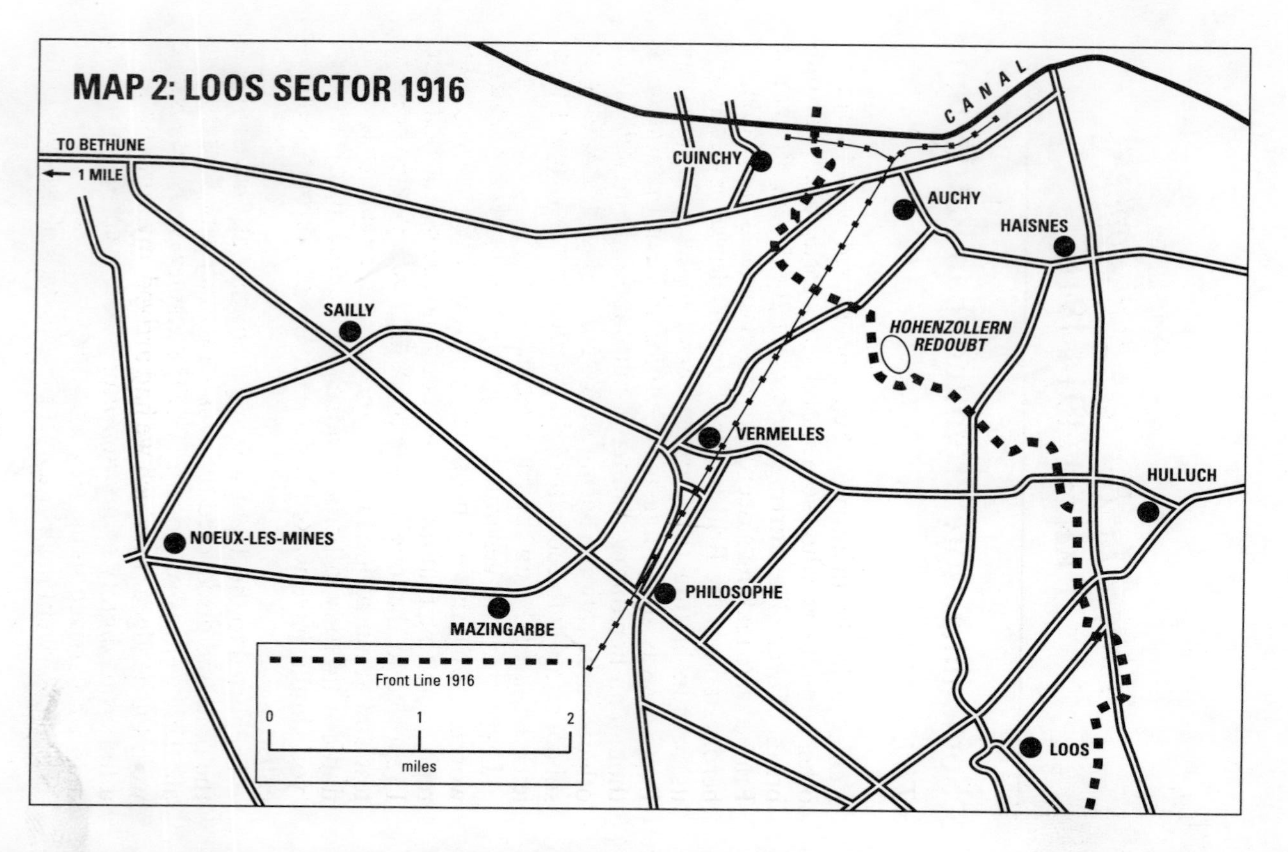
MAP 2: LOOS SECTOR 1916
TO BETHUNE
1 MILE
CANAL
CUINCHY
AUCHY
HAISNES
SAILLY
HOHENZOLLERN REDOUBT
VERMELLES
HULLUCH
NOEUX-LES-MINES
PHILOSOPHE
MAZINGARBE
Front Line 1916
0
1
2
miles
LOOS

Home – Le Havre – Philosophe – Vermelles – Loos

THE CALL

I enlisted in the infantry in September 1914 with the many other volunteers who were mobilised shortly after the outbreak of war. The stirring reports of the Great Retreat in France were making a deep impression on us, in particular the heroic stand of the British Expeditionary Force at Mons and its part in halting the German move to seize the Channel Ports. It was something more profound than patriotism, as though an hereditary instinct of nationhood had swept aside other considerations, daring our manhood and impelling us subconsciously to the battlefield. Whatever it was, many of us felt we must take up the challenge.

I wrote to the general manager of the bank for which I worked, resigning my position, and took little notice of his reply regretting that my request could not be met at that time. I reported to the local barracks, where I was given a medical test and accepted for military service. That evening I was to find out that my father was none too pleased at my action – 'you should have waited for a commission; only ex-convicts enlist!'

I reported to the depot wearing a bowler hat, fashionable at the time, and discovered that while there were uniforms for us all, there were as yet no caps. For the first few weeks we had to wear the headgear in which we had arrived, my bowler adding a ludicrous dignity to my uniform. It was even worse for the man who arrived in his straw boater!

We underwent healthy and strenuous days of training at the

British Military Camp at The Curragh. At the first flush of morning the trumpeters cantered past the crowded rows of tents pitched on the broad plain, sounding reveille for cavalry, gunners and infantry. The day's work started early as we formed up in our thousands and ended at 10 o'clock in the evening to the solemn strains of the *Last Post*.

We were confident that victory awaited us across the Channel, sure that this was to be the greatest event in our lives, in our country's history, making our peace-time activities seem insignificant in comparison with a call to defend our country. There were militia-men among us, wearing South African war ribbons, who were amused at the large body of civilians who had become soldiers overnight. They were always ready to make fun of any arduous drill and training which they thought to be unnecessary – for them anyway. This did not mean they were less keen than we but they did not see the war as the game we imagined it to be.

Soon we were formed into battalions, brigades and divisions, numbered among those who came to be known as 'The First Hundred Thousand' – Kitchener's citizen volunteer army. We were moved to barracks and camps in different parts of the country where we continued our programme of 10 to 12 hours instruction a day. Our training had worked wonders and we were soon in the pink of condition.

By Christmas 1914 I was wearing my third stripe, proud to be a member of the Sergeants' Mess. In the evenings we gathered around the mess table, carefree and elated, our faces brown, our pre-war days forgotten, comrades bound together by a common *esprit de corps*. We felt we knew something about war and considered ourselves trained soldiers. My battalion, the 8th Royal Inniskilling Fusiliers, was as good a unit as any Colonel would wish to command and we were as proud of him as he was of us.

I received my commission in April 1915 and was given command of a platoon. During a week's leave I acquired my new uniform and with it the braid and star insignia of an officer, a sword, a valise, items of bedding and a Sam Browne belt. Here I was, aged 23, my life greatly expanded, invested with new responsibilities, excited by the opportunities that lay ahead. It was no wonder I proudly showed off my new uniform to May, my sweetheart, in Tipperary, and to my parents. This did not mean that I was unfeeling of the tragedy of men being trained to fight against other men, but I saw our cause as compelling, provoked by Germany's ruthless onslaught against the helpless Belgians. My friends and I found something selfless, virtuous and even noble in our response.

FINAL PREPARATIONS

In the autumn we moved to Inkerman Barracks at Woking to join the many other divisions in that region. I was amazed at the sight of so many troops in training, especially in the Aldershot area. We were inspected by Queen Mary, the King having been invalided after a fall from his horse in France. It was an imposing sight, the long ranks of our Division stretching far into the distance, drawn up for the General Salute. It was not just a ceremonial review, it was 20,000 men who had volunteered to defend their country demonstrating their allegiance in the presence of Her Majesty before taking their place on the battlefield.

We were sent to Bordon Camp in Hampshire for the winter of 1915 where we trained even harder, covering 20 miles a day, skirmishing over difficult fen-type country. The enthusiasm and boyish elation of 1914 had now given place to a sterner attitude. The war had become dead-locked and our armies were immobile, exerted to the full in maintaining the defensive. The nature of our training had changed as the year progressed so as to adapt to the conditions we would encounter. We could now visualise the wasteful and dreary vigil of trench life and could see better what was likely to be required of us. It was still a great adventure but there was a realisation that no quick victory awaited us on the other side and we would need to develop and display qualities of endurance, self-denial and mental control.

We chafed at being told that the other two brigades of our

division were to set off for France, leaving our 49th Brigade at Bordon, but it was a relief to know that at last we must be getting near our goal.

THE WEDDING

The order putting us under a few weeks notice for France arrived not long after the other brigades had left and our enthusiasm swelled. Excitedly, I got in touch with May who, to my joy, came over from Tipperary. We decided to get married, discounting my parents' advice, and did so in Bordon Church on 22nd January 1916.

There could be no honeymoon as all leave had been stopped, but I was lucky to find board and lodging for her near the camp. In the evening after a day's training May would play the piano for a few of us as we gathered round and sang popular songs; *No Rose in All The World Until You Came, Sometimes Between Long Shadows On The Grass* and others. It was a brief three weeks; then it was over and May returned home.

TO FRANCE

We received our mobilisation orders for service overseas and within two weeks had completed our final preparations. We left Bordon for Southampton by train on the 20th February, embarking on the *SS Marguerite*. The sea was unusually rough and many of us were sick, made worse by there being barely room to stand. After six hours we turned back and anchored off Southampton.

The next night we made another attempt, this time successful, and disembarked at Le Havre in the early hours of the morning. We marched through the town and up a steep hill to the transit camp, arriving there before a heavy fall of snow.

I shared a tent the first night with several others, including my good pals Freddie Martin and Bill Ellis. The following afternoon we left Le Havre by train for Lillers, about 14 miles behind the front line in the Loos sector. It was still snowing as we made the weary four mile march from the station to our billets in a small village, where the men slept in barns and we shared spare rooms in cottages.

THE ROAD TO THE FRONT

The next day we left Lillers and marched towards the front. That evening I found myself sitting in a little French kitchen, eating an omelette, drinking coffee, glad of a comfortable billet, but all the time listening to the distant thunder of guns and wondering what lay ahead. It was afternoon the next day when we arrived close to the line and marched through Bethune on the road leading to the enemy-held town of Lens. We were in the heart of France's coal mining area, the flat landscape stretched out before us dotted with pits and slag heaps. Shells were falling on the road ahead, causing us to deploy into platoon formation to reduce the risk of casualties, and we went forward keeping our distance.

In the evening we settled into the half-ruined hamlet of Philosophe, the gun area, where the air pounded with the incessant firing of our artillery followed by the distant explosions of their shells. The country in front of us was derelict and deserted, uncultivated fields scarred with shell holes. We knew we had reached the war.

The house in which Freddie Martin and I shared a room was intact apart from having no glass in the windows. After dark we watched the ghostly rise and fall of Very lights which marked the front line, about four miles or so ahead of us. Every now and then activity would flare up in a different part of the line, a rapid bombardment usually accompanied by machine-gun and rifle fire, the dull thuds of exploding shells dying away as quickly as they had begun, only to be repeated a short time later elsewhere along the front.

We had been issued with the new type steel helmet, long capes, sheepskin waistcoats and thigh gumboots. In the morning my platoon and one from another company prepared to go up on our first tour of the trenches. We 'fell-in' with feelings of excitement and apprehension and marched slowly along the road to Vermelles, heavily laden with clothing and equipment. The devastation around us became worse as we went along, small wooden crosses on each side of the road marking the graves of many who had gone before us. There was a good deal of enemy shelling, to which our guns, concealed in ruins on each side of the road, barked out their reply. It seemed to us at that time strange, though soon to become commonplace, to hear hidden guns firing at an unseen foe.

THE 'TRENCHMAN'

The 6th Cameron Highlanders were holding the central section of the line in front of Hulluch just north of the town of Loos. They sent a soldier to meet us on the outskirts of the ruined village of Vermelles, to act as our guide through the long and tortuous labyrinth of trenches – communication trenches – leading to his battalion's position. His chin displayed several days' bristle, the pallor of his gaunt face accentuated by specks of chalk from the trenches, his muddy uniform covered in white streaks. This was 'the trenchman', a distinctive product of the war; silent, strained, tired, yet with a look in his eyes that showed a keen alertness to his surroundings, always watching and listening. I felt as a child in his presence.

We followed in single file into the narrow trench which started its course on the outskirts of Vermelles a mile or so back from the front. The trench became noticeably narrower and deeper as we trudged along until in places it was only just possible to squeeze past the chalky sides. At first there were duckboards but soon we found ourselves wading through several inches of thick pasty water. We continued on for what seemed hours, shells bursting around us, the water creeping up to our knees. Our escort confided that the enemy strafe was unusually heavy that day, which was probably meant to reassure us; but somehow it didn't.

At last our guide led us into a trench branching off from the communication trench, which was the support line, several hundred yards behind the forward positions. Here we found ourselves among small groups of Cameron Highlanders, dirty and tired, but cheerful. Some were standing around little charcoal braziers, appearing to get some heat from them, others were cooking slabs of bacon in their mess-tins.

At the side of the trench I saw an opening about 3-foot square which our Scotsman told me was Company Headquarters. I arranged for my platoon to be spread out along the line and I went through the opening. I was at the top of a shaft with steps descending steeply to a depth of about 50 feet. With difficulty I climbed down and found myself in a sizeable subterranean room. I was at last in the legendary 'dugout'. It was one of the deep excavations for which this particular sector was renowned, constructed by the Germans in the early stages of the war and captured by our troops at the Battle of Loos in September 1915. A large table stood on the rough chalk floor, around which several officers were sitting. I introduced myself and was invited to join them for the end of what had obviously been a good tea. I thought to myself that perhaps the war was not so bad after all.

THE FRONT AT LAST

After a briefing by the Company Commander I left the support line, again accompanied by my Scottish friend, and led my platoon up to the front, ploughing our way through more thick mud and water. Our guide sometimes stopped abruptly, gazed fixedly at the sky, ducked in anticipation of the explosion which moments later occurred close by. If my platoon and I showed indifference to the danger during those first few days it was due to our ignorance of the characteristics of the rifle grenade, that detestable weapon which later caused us so many casualties. It did not take long before we too were able to detect the approach of that conveyor of death, by day anyway, to predict its flight and take avoiding action. After dark it was a different matter, the grenade posed a more serious threat and it took us longer to acquire skill in dealing with that menace.

I watched the sentries in the front line as they stood motionless, their eyes rivetted on small mirrors positioned at the top of the trench, enabling them to observe a wide sector of no-man's-land. A mirror was smashed by a sniper's bullet as I watched, to be immediately replaced. I looked through one of these instruments and saw several forms hanging over our barbed wire about 30 yards in front of us, which must have been there for some time, their uniforms alone identifying them as bodies.

Later on, when darkness fell, soldiers seemed to appear from everywhere and take up their positions. The sentries mounted the fire-steps and leant forward with their heads just high enough above the top of the trench to enable them to peer out. For the first time I was witnessing the regular evening 'stand-to' at the front. Our machine-guns began raking no-man's-land and the enemy trench with repeated bursts, provoking the Germans, in some places no more than 150 yards away, to return an equally unwelcome compliment.

THE FIRST ENCOUNTER

As darkness fell an enemy patrol succeeded in creeping up to the Cameronians' wire and threw a shower of bombs at one of our sentry groups in a sap – a small trench dug forward from the front line to our own wire. These saps were only manned after dark, the risk of having soldiers there in daylight being too great. In this instance the enemy was driven off by our machine-guns and we suffered only light casualties.

During the night the Cameronians themselves planned to carry out a small raid. The preliminaries opened with a roar of gunfire behind us, the whistling of shells overhead, followed almost instantaneously by dull explosions along the enemy line. Within moments a salvo of Very lights shot skywards from the enemy front, the battlefield was lit by an eerie brightness. Every machine-gun in the vicinity, on both sides, seemed to be spitting out its bullets, all this against a background of deep rending explosions – the unmistakable sound of trench mortars. It was an awesome thought for us newcomers that in the middle of this inferno of bombs, bullets and shell, and under these ghastly gleams, men were killing and being killed.

We moved back to the support trench, where to begin with, we were in a good position to witness the night's drama. It was not to be for long because enemy artillery soon forced us to take cover. We had to move again, this time a little further back, but still to a position from where we could watch events.

The moment had now arrived for the Cameronians to raid the German lines. They set off across no-man's-land, which all the time was being swept by bullets, was riddled with shell holes, reeking of death, interlaced with endless strands of wire which appeared in the gloom like grotesque undergrowth. The foray ended with our troops hurling their bombs into the enemy trench. Now they had the difficult task of getting back to the comparative safety of their own lines, not just themselves, but with their wounded. The dead might have to wait.

My men and I stayed for the rest of the night in the trench under improvised shelters. I was with a Scottish subaltern, crouching under an inadequate roof consisting of a groundsheet. It did not even stop thawed snow from dripping on us. The third occupant of the shelter was the subaltern's batman, due to go on leave to 'Blighty' in the morning, whose eyes seemingly shone as his thoughts and words dwelt on his home in the Highlands. He would not at that moment have changed places with the King.

The next day was bright and sunny and we were not sorry at being ordered to rejoin the battalion at Philosophe. As we made our way back along the communication trenches an aerial combat took place immediately overhead. An enemy squadron appeared at high altitude, just specks in the sun, descending rapidly as they approached our lines. Our anti-aircraft guns, or 'archies', engaged them. Black bursts appeared in the sky above us, followed by the sound of falling shell fragments, making us thankful for our steel helmets. Then we saw several of our planes spring out of a cloud, like bolts from the blue, nose-dive at speed and swoop past the enemy planes with machine-guns firing. The opposing formations were quick to divide, became separated by the whole expanse of sky, all but one enemy plane which burst into flames and fell to the ground like an expiring meteor.

We had a good evening back in Philosophe recounting our experiences to the fellows who had not yet had their baptism of fire. There had been one casualty in our absence – the first in our battalion.

Matthew's battalion was now in the Loos Sector. It had been the scene of a British attack the previous September, one of the earliest Allied offensives of the year. The attack had made good headway on the first day, our troops occupied the town of Loos and seized the ground beyond as far as the Hulluch road. The Hohenzollern Redoubt, an intricate system of enemy trenches about two miles north of Loos, was also captured. Seasoned German troops, strongly reinforced the next day, halted our advance and counter-attacked, causing us heavy losses. A number of units of Kitchener's 'First 100,000', recently arrived in France, were engaged in the assault.

For the next three weeks there was virtually deadlock, the troops experiencing some of the fiercest hand-to-hand fighting of the war. The trenches in the Hohenzollern Redoubt changed hands several times before finally being regained by the enemy. Towards the closing stages of the battle a determined enemy counter-attack along the whole front was repulsed leaving the British in possession of the Loos Salient. It was one of the most severely contested battles of the war.

No major offensives were undertaken by either side

during the time Matthew was in this sector. He was to experience the life of a soldier in what has been described as 'routine trench warfare'.

HOLDING THE LINE

Each platoon was attached in turn for similar instruction at the front. Soon our 16th Division was allotted its own part of the line and we took over the salient around Loos, which was to become our sector for some time. The front line ran about a thousand yards or so beyond the town, with the close support trench along the back of it, through the gardens of houses reduced to low jagged walls and piles of bricks.

We were soon to become familiar with the vast network of trenches, most with nicknames, '10th Avenue', 'Vendin Alley', all of which we got to know better than we knew the streets of our home towns. We acquired an intimate knowledge of the line, the danger zones, the safer spots, the places where rifle grenades made life hell, the exposed and dangerous corners of trenches where snipers claimed their daily toll, the areas where the unwary could be caught by trench mortars. In no-man's-land we knew those parts where the survival chances of a patrol or wiring party were slim. All these were soon to become second nature to us; we were old campaigners now.

In some cases the cellars of houses were used as dugouts, strengthened overhead and made more shell-proof by heaps of bricks and rubble. Often as we sat around the mess table a terrific crash would resound overhead, putting out all the candles and causing everything to shake. We were safe on those occasions so long as the roof held; somehow it always did. We also had the old German dugouts, built by them during their earlier occupation, which were deep and spacious, for which we were very thankful.

We were not in the front line continuously but rotated our duties according to a sequence with which we were to become familiar. A spell of four days at the front would be followed by four in '10th Avenue' in support, then four in close reserve, and finally four in reserve back in our transport lines. How we looked forward to those four days in reserve in rest billets, tempered by the knowledge that they would soon be followed by a long and tedious journey back to Loos and four days in the front line. To begin with the rest area was in the ruins of Philosophe but it became so 'unhealthy' that we moved to the neighbouring village of Mazingarbe which attracted less attention from enemy guns and where we were glad to find houses in better condition. Each tour in the forward area was paid for in flesh and blood, new faces would appear in the ranks, familiar ones would become a memory.

In addition to my platoon I was in charge of a section of our battalion Lewis gunners. One afternoon I had just led my gun team back from the front into rest billets at Mazingarbe to rejoin the company when the enemy put down a bombardment on the village itself and on the roads immediately leading out. It was a new experience for us to be subjected to heavy shelling without the protection of a trench and we felt unusually exposed. A bombardment such as this on the back areas usually meant that the enemy was about to attack and were attempting to prevent us from sending up reinforcements.

Within an hour I received an order to return to the front with my gun team, the enemy were carrying out a large raid from the famous Hohenzollern Redoubt, a strongpoint in the German line consisting of a maze of trenches. I assembled my party at the edge of Mazingarbe and waited for a short time while shells continued to fall about a 100 yards or so ahead of us and along the main route leading out to Philosophe.

I took my gun team with me and looked for another way out. I found a track leading towards the front which was not being heavily shelled and despite giving us a longer journey offered a better chance of getting to where we were needed with our guns. We waited for a lull in the shelling immediately in front and set off, carrying the heavy Lewis guns, loaded magazines and tool kits, keeping clear of the more commonly used paths leading up to the line. We made our way as quickly as we could and fortunately did not encounter any more serious shelling, reaching the front at 10 pm without suffering any casualties. Our line had held out against the attack in the afternoon and we were now preparing for a continuation of the raid that night. I set up our two Lewis guns. We were in action on and off throughout the night, an anxious one, as the whole line was jumpy, each side straffing the other with everything it could at the slightest sign of any activity on their part.

The enemy's artillery and supply of shells, however, exceeded ours and he could blow us out of our trenches without much fear of effective retaliation. We had to rely mainly on rifle grenades and machine-guns. It was flesh and blood against metal and that night metal won. When morning came our trenches were practically unrecognisable; our medical staff and burying parties were kept busy. But we were still in possession of the line.

I was ordered back to Mazingarbe and we set off again, carrying the heavy Lewis guns and their equipment. My weary team needed all the encouragement I could give them while we made the long march back. Finally we reached the village shortly after midnight, having had no sleep for over 24 hours. The men went to their hut, but I did not fancy my chances of finding a billet at that hour of the night so I flung myself down in a stable in the transport lines with my overcoat between me and the ground. I slept soundly but woke up frozen.

REFUGE IN A MINE SHAFT

Several weeks later we again had to move our battalion transport lines and quartermaster stores because of continuing enemy shelling. This time they went to Noeux-les-Mines, a mining town further to the rear, connected by rail to Bethune. It made a good billet area, situated in comparative civilisation. When our turn came for a few days in reserve, it was a joy to get back there from the line, to find little cafes and pianos, good enough wine, a cinema in an old barn, and better than anything, beds with sheets. Thoughts of its pleasures seemed to sing in our minds and warmed our spirits as we happily toiled the five miles rearwards. It was quite different on the return, the journey back to the Loos Salient always seemed to take much longer.

We still went back to battered Philosophe when in close reserve. On one occasion I happened to be there with my platoon after an extended tour in the line when I was unexpectedly told to take them back to the front the next morning to provide a working party for the Engineers. By now I had discovered that a large part of life in the trenches consisted of the irksome task of taking charge of working parties. We started off shortly after dawn, the men with their rifles, bayonets and ammunition, all of us relieved at the welcome change of being so lightly burdened. It was a lovely morning with the sun shining and spring in the air.

These parties were often used to assist the miners who were working at the front or close to it. This time my platoon was ordered to help a Tunnelling Company of Engineers who had just dug a gallery extending from our trench to a position under the enemy line and were now ready to instal the explosives. I was walking back along a shallow trench towards my party, who were waiting nearby, when a shell landed a few yards in front of me, flattening out the trench on each side. By some miracle I remained unscathed. The enemy had obviously seen us arrive because a few moments later they fired a volley of rifle grenades. By now we had been at the front long enough to look out for these deadly devices and needed no prompting to hurry away from their expected point of impact and stay put until the firing had stopped. Worse was to come.

The explosives, packed in large biscuit tins, were stacked some distance away and had to be carried along the trench to the mouth of the shaft. To do this we would have to traverse a 50 yard stretch of trench which had been almost completely blown in. Any movement by us along it could easily be observed by the enemy, who were only 200 yards away. The best chance of getting the job done quickly seemed to me to be to divide into groups of two and three, collect the tins, make for the exposed section, and scamper across it as quickly as possible during lulls in the firing.

I led my party to the stack of explosives where each man picked up a heavy two-foot square tin and put it on his shoulder. We started back along the narrow trench towards the dangerous section where the first party clambered up and staggered across it with their heavy tins. The enemy had seen us and before the rest of us could get across a heavy bombardment fell along the trench, this time artillery shells. Two of my men were wounded.

There was no dugout anywhere near so I ordered my platoon to leave the tins for the time being in the trench and run as fast as they could to the mine shaft, helping the two wounded along with them. We scuttled across like rabbits and down the entrance. Not only had we been spotted but the large biscuit tins would have revealed what we were doing. The exact positions of our mine shafts were well known to the Germans and the bombardment continued. We stayed huddled together at the mouth of the shaft, which narrowed too sharply for us to descend further, expecting the shelling soon to stop so that we could finish transporting the explosives.

We heard a roar from the bottom of the shaft, it was the Mining Officer shouting to us to get out of the mine entrance because there was not enough air where he and his miners were working. He would have been unaware of the tremendous fire now crashing down on the remains of the trenches immediately outside. I put him right on that, somewhat bluntly, and during a heated conversation added several home-truths for good measure. I did not intend that we should be cut to pieces to enable him and his miners to breathe more freely. We stayed where we were, squeezed up together.

No one spoke, all of us must have been praying that a shell would not score a direct hit on the parapet immediately above us, or worse still, on the entrance to the shaft. The choice lay between being buried alive or being killed by fragments. I was sitting just inside the entrance and in the best position to see what was happening during that half-hour while hell raged all around us. The trench was churned up, parts of it were flattened, mounds of earth piled up on each side.

The shelling stopped as abruptly as it had started. The entrance to the mine shaft had escaped. We found stretchers for our wounded and took them to the nearby First Aid Post. Sadly, for one of them it looked to be too late. The mining operation was suspended until after dark. I collected my platoon together and we carefully made our way back through the broken ground, seeing evidence all around us of considerable casualties to the trench garrison who had remained at their posts during the bombardment, losing eight men killed and a number wounded.

We reached Philosophe in record time, where I had much to tell the other fellows in the Company Mess, not noticing that at the same time I was making substantial inroads into their day's whisky supply!

EASTER SUNDAY

We were on our way back to the line one day in April, having completed our rest period in Noeux-les-Mines, when we reached the place near Philosophe where the road crossed a railway line alongside two mines and their slag heaps. We were in the usual march formation of platoons in file at intervals of about 50 yards. The crossing was being shelled as I approached at the head of my platoon. I saw a gunner and his horse struck, the horse leaping a low hedge and falling dead in the field, while the man fell to the ground and was carried off by his comrades.

Lieut-Colonel Walton, our Commanding Officer, was on his horse at a dangerous spot, encouraging us all. I had a great admiration for him, his bravery, his leadership and his friendliness. I was on the point of crossing the railway when I heard a shell coming, sounding like a fast train approaching through a tunnel, the noise growing greater and greater. It gave me the usual shrinking sensation, a sickening feeling in the stomach, one of the worst effects I endured under shelling. I stopped in my tracks, remained frozen in an upright position. A moment later there was a shattering crash and a shell burst on the road not more than ten yards in front of me, its fragments whistling past my face. I looked around and saw that my men, sensibly, had thrown themselves flat on the ground, where fortunately none had been hit. I needed no further encouragement to move on quickly. A moment later we heard another shell explode and without slacking pace I looked back and saw it had fallen on almost the same spot where I had been standing.

By early evening we were trudging up the communication trench, 'Vendin Alley', on the last leg of the trek back to the front. When dawn broke the sky was beautiful to look at, refreshing our trench-weary eyes. Then I remembered, it was Sunday, Easter Sunday, 1916.

THE BATTALION DECIMATED

A few days later the Medical Officer told me to report to the Military Hospital at Bethune to have treatment for several boils which had broken out on my head and were causing me considerable pain. From Bethune I was sent on to a hospital at Rouen, about 35 miles east of the port of Le Havre, where I had first landed in France in February. The doctor detained me at the hospital for treatment.

I heard a few days later that the morning after I had left the Loos sector the enemy had sent over a gas cloud and behind it had launched a heavy attack on our lines. The division suffered 1,200 casualties, my 8th Battalion was decimated, losing five officers and many good men killed and a large number wounded or incapacitated by gas.

WELCOMED BACK

It was six weeks before I was discharged from hospital and set off from Rouen to rejoin my battalion. I made my way back to Mazingarbe where I found the Quartermaster. After dark I went up with him to the front, through Philosophe to 'The Crucifix' in Loos, plodding along the maze of communication trenches which ran through the ruined buildings, until we reached battalion headquarters on the far side of the town. I went down into a deep one-time German dugout to report to Colonel Walton. He welcomed me back in the kindest of terms, making me prouder than ever to serve under him, and told me to take command of 'A' Company pending the return of their commander.

On reaching the front I came face to face with a weird figure who had just come round a corner in the trench. He was holding a revolver in his right hand and a Very light pistol in his left, his face looking exceptionally pale and haggard in the moonlight. This was the customary gear of the officer-on-watch. Standing in front of me was my dear old friend Bill Ellis who had shortly before won the Military Cross for gallantry in charge of a patrol.

We greeted each other warmly. He told me about the action during the time I was away, the death of many old comrades and the horrors of the gas attack. Apparently one gas cloud was greenish, followed by a yellow one. Fortunately the wind veered and some of the poison gas was blown back towards the enemy lines, enabling our fellows to derive some satisfaction from seeing the German ambulances arrive to collect their own gassed casualties.

MY FIRST PATROL

I received orders almost immediately to prepare for a large scale raid that the battalion would be carrying out the following night. The assault wave was to be provided by the Company on my immediate right but the orders for the raid involved us too; almost every man in our unit had a role to play in the attack.

On the night itself a mine was exploded under the German line immediately opposite, the signal for our raiding party to move as quickly as they could across no-man's-land and seize the enemy trench. Our artillery put down a barrage on each side and to the rear of the enemy trench to prevent its occupants either escaping or being reinforced. Simultaneously two parties began digging shallow trenches from our front line forward to the lip of the new crater to help us move up further troops and equipment to consolidate any ground gained and if possible push forward our line by the width of no-man's-land that night.

My task was to remain in the trench with several others, including Bill Ellis and the Company Sergeant-Major, and deceive the enemy into believing our front line was fully manned so as to dissuade him from launching a counter-raid that could disrupt our attack. Armed with rifles we moved quickly up and down the trench firing rounds at frequent intervals from different places. To begin with this was easy and seemed almost humorous, but the Boche soon put down a heavy retaliatory bombardment which nearly blew us out of our position. We bore charmed lives that night; in less than an hour our trench was a mass of loose soil and broken duck-boards.

Meanwhile the action in front of us was being successfully fought. Most of the enemy in the raided sector had been accounted for, their dugouts bombed and a few prisoners taken. Our troops withdrew to the edge of the crater, bringing back their casualties. By this time the enemy had sent for reinforcements and mounted a counter-attack. This led to a fierce hand-to-hand combat with bayonets and bombs around the crater, lasting almost until dawn. Our troops held their ground. Much to our sorrow we learnt that the officer who had led the raid so gallantly had been badly wounded and had died shortly afterwards in his dugout, to which he had been carried by his faithful batman.

While this second phase of the battle was in progress I was ordered to take out a patrol and find out if the enemy were occupying one of their saps directly in front of us. Some of my men had now returned to me from other activities in support of the raid and I chose three reliable fellows. We sallied forth on our first patrol, the men armed with rifles and bombs. It was difficult getting under our own wire but once through it we were able to move more easily, worming our way in and out of shell holes and through any dark vegetation, but always hugging the ground. Again and again enemy machine-guns fired in our direction, cutting off the tops of the grass in which we lay, a forcible reminder to us to remain motionless in no-man's-land each time a Very light burst in the air. As we groped our way forward we had to keep our ears open to avoid an unexpected confrontation with a German patrol.

We reached a position close to the enemy sap and there we heard their voices and could see the tops of their helmets. The trench was strongly manned. On our way back to report we watched an aeroplane make a forced landing in no-man's-land some distance away, where it was immediately shelled and caught fire.

In the morning the bodies of eight of our men killed during the night were taken past. They were being borne on the shoulders of the carrying party because all available stretchers were needed for the twenty or so wounded.

POIGNANT BEAUTY

One day in summer I was making my way along the support line in the town of Loos and found myself looking at the poppies and cornflowers hanging in festoons from the top of the trenches dug through the one-time gardens of the shattered houses. I remembered how bleak and bare everything had looked at the time we arrived here towards the end of winter and were first shown those trenches. Now the scene looked different, one of poignant beauty.

THE GERMAN MINE

My earlier experience with the Tunnelling Company, when I demanded refuge in their mine, did not in any way diminish my admiration and respect for the miners. They could find themselves working at the bottom of a narrow shaft, with barely room to move their bodies, when they might hear a tap-

tap close to them. It would almost certainly be the sound of an enemy pick sinking a counter-shaft. This meant that the enemy intended either to destroy the gallery in which our miner was working by springing a mine underneath it, or to break into the shaft and attack him. Either prospect was dreaded by the tunneller as he was perhaps 100 feet under ground, in a confined space, breathing bad air and relying solely on a candle for lighting. Should the tapping stop the wisest course would be for him to clear out quickly. No wonder some of these brave men became old overnight.

Late one evening we had got back to Noeux-les-Mines when word came we were to take over a new part of the line next morning as the 15th Division, then on our left flank, were moving out. We were to man the stretch known as 'Church Alley', which ran uncomfortably close to the strongly fortified Hohenzollern Redoubt. On arriving at this new position the outgoing unit cheerfully told us that the Germans had tunnelled under the middle of our line and the mine must by now be ready to go up!

The support trench, which was unmanned, was several hundred yards behind the front line and connected to it at intervals by communication trenches. Under the circumstances we thought it better not to spread out along the whole of the front line trench but to man it only with sentry groups stationed at its junctions with the communication trenches.

That night the Company Commander and myself were the only officers available, the other subaltern had been recalled to battalion headquarters. The job of the officer-on-watch was to walk up and down the company front line trench, visit the sentry groups and supervise any working parties which were out that night. The spell was usually 2 hours on and 4 hours off, but on this occasion, because there were only two of us, it fell to me to do the whole night and have the morning to sleep it off. I walked above the mine feeling as though I were making my way around the edge of a volcano which was about to erupt, except that now I found myself assessing the odds of being blown over the German line when the time came or having the good luck to land behind our own.

The mine went up on the fourth day, and with it, tragically, almost half the company which had just relieved us.

NEWS OF THE SOMME

Various courses of instruction were being held and I was nominated to attend a Company Commander's course for six weeks starting in August. I travelled back to the delightful village of Condette, between Boulogne and Hardelot, where I reported to the Commandant of the First Army School, located in the nearby chateau. It was a pleasant change from the trenches and, although we worked hard, there was some time for recreation, even swimming at Hardelot Plage.

Whilst there, I heard that my battalion had been moved from Loos to the Somme three weeks after I had left for my course. I now knew why we had taken over that mined trench near the Hohenzollern Redoubt; to enable the troops previously there to be transferred to the Somme. Now my 8th Battalion was there too.

Shortly afterwards news came through of a great battle on the Somme, where our 16th Division had distinguished itself in the capture of Guillemont and Ginchy. Guillemont had been twice captured, first by the Royal Scots and several days later by the West Lancashire Division, only to be driven back on each occasion, finally to be recaptured and held in a combined attack in which the Inniskilling Fusiliers took part. The price paid by my battalion on the Somme had been terrible, with over 200 men killed, wounded and missing and nearly 20 casualties among the officers. I was greatly saddened to hear that our commending officer, Lieut-Colonel Walton, had been killed. To me he had been an inspiration and I knew I would never forget him.

Lieut-Colonel Hubert Pulteney Dalzell-Walton, Mentioned in Despatches, died on 9th September 1916, age 50. He had previously served in the Bechuanaland Expedition 1884-1885, in the Burma War 1886-1889 in which he was twice wounded, and in the South African War. He was the son of Hubert Izaak Walton, Director-General of Telegraphs in Bombay and the Persian Gulf. His grave lies in a military cemetery on the Somme, near Albert.

When the course ended I set off to rejoin my battalion, now on its way back from the battle, and shortly before midnight arrived at Sailly-le-Sec, a small village on the River Somme near Amiens. I was standing at a cross-roads in the centre of the village when I picked up the sound of drums and fifes in the distance. It was my poor old 8th Battalion, weary and worn, marching towards the village. I rejoined them, to find myself among many new faces. It was heart-rending to see so many gaps that could never be filled.

Shortly afterwards we received our movement orders. We were to be transferred from France to Flanders. Buses took us to Pont Remy, 5 miles south east of Abbeville, and from there we went by train to Bailleul - the last French town before Belgium. Less than 10 miles to the north lay Ypres, the famous war-torn town in Flanders about which I had heard so much since 1914, in whose defence the British Army had won such renown.

PART 2 1916-1917

'Ready to Do what was Expected'

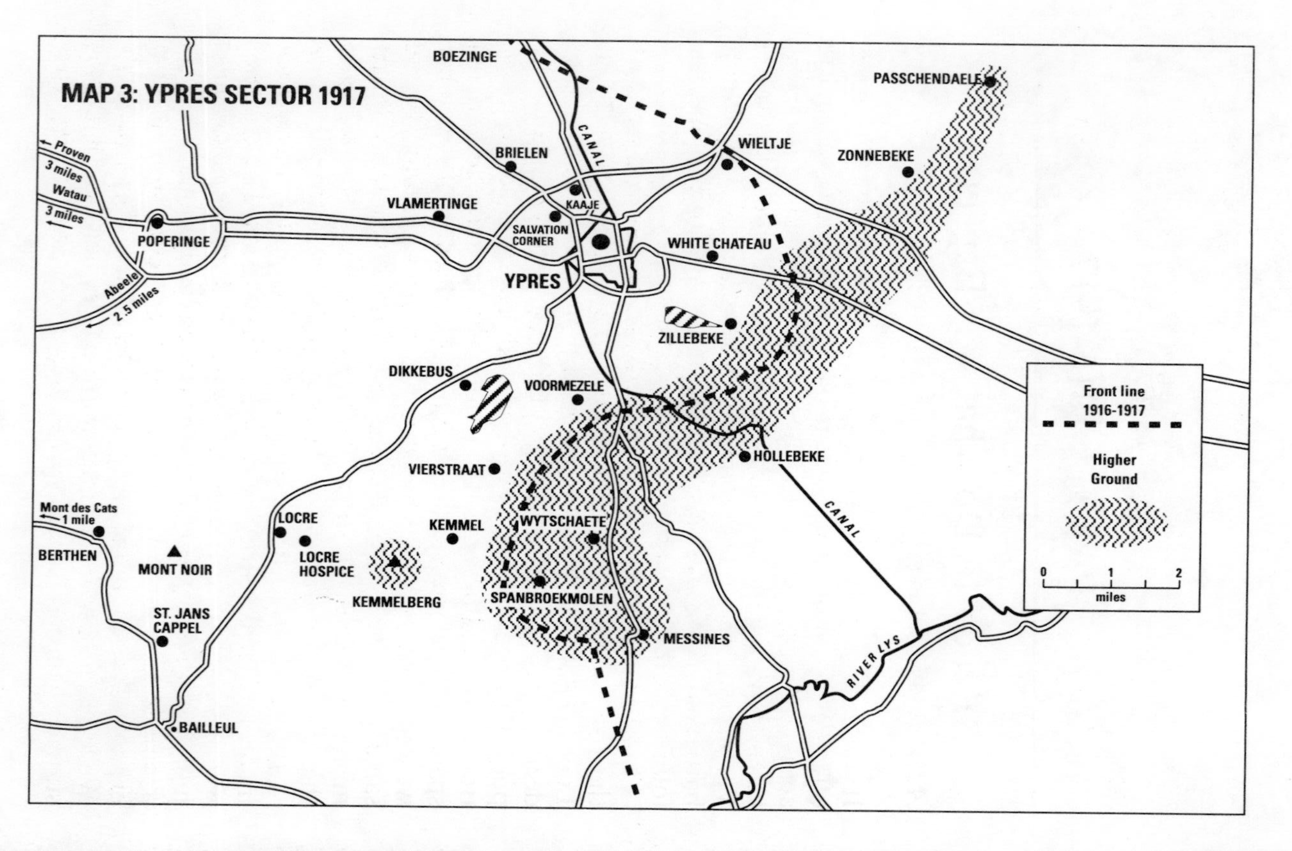
MAP 3: YPRES SECTOR 1917
BOEZINGE
PASSCHENDAELE
CANAL
WIELTJE
ZONNEBEKE
BRIELEN
Proven
3 miles
Watau
3 miles
VLAMERTINGE
KAAJE
SALVATION CORNER
POPERINGE
WHITE CHATEAU
YPRES
Abeele
2.5 miles
ZILLEBEKE
DIKKEBUS
VOORMEZELE
Front line 1916-1917
Higher Ground
HOLLEBEKE
VIERSTRAAT
CANAL
Mont des Cats
1 mile
LOCRE
KEMMEL
WYTSCHAETE
BERTHEN
MONT NOIR
LOCRE HOSPICE
KEMMELBERG
SPANBROEKMOLEN
0 1 2
miles
ST. JANS CAPPEL
MESSINES
RIVER LYS
BAILLEUL

Locre – Kemmel – Messines – Ypres

ARRIVAL YPRES

It was nearly midnight when we detrained at Bailleul and set off over the cobble-stones of the old town on the road leading across the Belgian border to Locre. We marched for six miles, listening all the time to the sounds of war and looking at the Very lights, reminders that we were again getting near a battlefield. When we reached the small town of Kemmel we found it badly damaged and almost deserted.

In front of the town lay a network of trenches leading up to the front. They were constructed differently from those at Loos because the wet ground made it impossible to dig down deeper than a few feet. The defences were completed by putting up breastworks, a wall of sandbags, on each side of the trench. At first this seemed to us much better than the confined spaces of the deep trenches we had been used to at Loos, but we soon realised that they did not afford anything like the same protection. We suffered casualties even from 'near-misses' as a result of the protective walls being blown in and the sides of the trenches collapsing in the soft ground.

To start with life in the sector was quiet, except for increasing enemy straffing with trench-mortars. These bombs were about two feet long, six inches in diameter, filled with high explosive and shot from the trench high into the air from a small hand-gun. We could see them coming and with experience could judge fairly accurately where they would fall. We found it best to wait until they had reached their apex and started their descent before deciding which way to run. That gave us about 3 or 4 seconds to bolt round a corner in the trench and lie down. A complication arose in this game if the bomb was fired from a position very much to the flank, or if it was coming out of the sun, or if two were fired at the same time from different directions. Some of us became adept at this sport, and lived, others were not so fortunate. As one fellow aptly put it: 'it's a case of the quick or the dead'.

LOCRE HOSPICE

After six days in the line we usually returned to the camp in Locre – 'Doncaster Huts'. There was a large convent on the edge of the town, Locre Hospice, a fine building used by the Nuns as a school. They also ran an Officers' Mess for battalions resting in the area, using lay workers to help them serve excellently cooked meals with good wine, at reasonable prices. One of the rooms was fitted with baths, a great luxury after living in the trenches and wearing the same clothes for six days and nights.

I am sure I will always remember the happy occasions in that large and well heated Mess, around the table after dinner, the scene more and more resembling a concert as the considerable entertaining talent that always seemed available was revealed. We were warm and friendly to one another, greatly valuing and depending on our comradeship in the trenches and at the same time making the best of any comfort we could find. One or two friends at our last gathering might now no longer be with us, their luck had run out, but we had to be fatalists and live for the present.

When we were at Locre we often made up a party and rode into Bailleul, where the shops were good, there was a large canteen and an Officers' Club. We would have a fine dinner and a merry time, galloping back without a care.

THE GLORY HOLE

In the centre of our new line was the famous 'Glory hole' where we knew great deeds had been performed at the Battle of Ypres in 1914 when an heroic band held it in desperate fighting and considerable sacrifice. It was on our left flank where the trench ran down into a valley, climbed a small hill on the opposite side, then jutted forward to a point at the top of the hill within thirty yards of the enemy line. This extremity was the 'Glory Hole', one of the key links in the defensive chain that stopped the German drive to the Channel Ports which threatened the British Expeditionary Force at that time. One afternoon I walked along the trench to take a quick look at this historic place, where, to my surprise, I found no sentry group in position. A little further on I saw a lot of blood in the trench and almost fell over a body. I then came across a soldier who told me that his officer and five men had been hit by a well-aimed and sudden shower of rifle grenades, killing the officer and two of the men. I sent for help from their headquarters and did what I could for the survivors.

WINTER LOOMS

It was now autumn and getting cold, with the prospect of a winter in the trenches. A question which arose was how to stop our feet from becoming frostbitten. The main preventive was to ensure that each man in the trench had a daily change of socks and rubbed his feet with a preparation of whale oil. Perhaps the issue of the rum ration was an even better precaution, which it often fell to me to dispense. At stand-to I used to go up with a large jug and a small glass measure, my batman following behind carrying a two-gallon jar of rum, 40% over proof. The men would look blue with cold as I passed along the trench giving each man his tot, and I have to say that no sacrament ever produced more visible results in the recipients; their drawn faces quickly revived with life and warmth.

I took over command of the company temporarily when Freddie Martin had to go to hospital with trench-fever, a disease causing pains in the joints. On going up to the front one evening I heard the good news that at the end of our six days there I would be due to go home on leave. It was now October, 1916, which meant that I had completed 9 months and would soon be seeing 'dear old Blighty' again. What a wonderful thought, except that six days lay ahead which had to be got through, within shouting distance of the 'gentle Hun'. The sentiments of a favourite ditty echoed in my head:

'I want to go Home! I want to go Home!
The bullets and shrapnel they whistle and roar,
I don't want to go to the front any more.
Take me over the sea, where the Alleyman can't get at me,
Oh my! I don't want to die! I want to go Home!'

A RAID EXPECTED

This tour at the front immediately before my leave was for me critical; the first few days went slowly and without much incident. I supervised the repair and drainage of trenches, organised wiring parties, arranged night patrols, slept for a few hours in the morning, dodged trench mortars, rang the artillery when retaliation was required and maintained the defence of my immediate stretch of line. On the last day things began to happen when I heard from headquarters that the enemy would probably raid my line that night. I had only 48 men in my depleted company and more than half a mile frontage to hold. During the afternoon three of my men were wounded, one by a sniper, the other two by a rifle grenade. The left flank of my position rested on the 'Glory Hole', where that night I positioned half of my small force, with as much ammunition, including bombs, as could be collected. I formed another strong post on the right flank with the remainder of the men and arranged for one NCO and two men to patrol the long strip of intervening trench. If the enemy attacked I would be able to concentrate my fire on them from the two positions.

We were on the *qui vive* that night. At midnight I was told that the 36th Ulster Division, immediately to our right, planned to release gas at 2 am. I thought to myself that I would prefer the enemy raid. When the time came I ordered my Company to put on respirators in case the wind should change. The gas was released from large cylinders which had been put in the line some time before to await favourable conditions. The hissing sound of discharging gas was almost drowned by machine-gun fire.

Moments later, as expected, enemy coloured Very lights soared up into the sky to warn their back areas of the gas attack and to call up their artillery. Shells soon crashed all around us, interspersed with heavy trench mortar bombs. As was customary on such occasions, our guns joined in and all hell reigned for several hours. Being in the front line and close to the enemy we were mostly showered with mortar bombs, the support line getting the shelling. It was not possible to see the mortar bombs at night but we were able to follow their flight by the faint thin trail of sparks emanating from the lighted fuse at the back, which just gave us time to take avoiding action. Through it all I thought of my coming leave and waited for the dawn. The expected enemy raid did not come off.

As day broke things quietened down. In the afternoon it was indeed with relief that I caught sight of the relieving company making their way up the communication trenches. As soon as the handover was complete we filed slowly along the front line trench for about a mile, myself at the rear, passing the 'Glory Hole'. To me anyway it seemed that no column had ever moved so slowly out of a front line. At last we reached 'Kitchen Alley', the communication trench, and I turned homewards, with my thoughts:

> 'It's a long way to Tipperary,
> It's a long way to go;
> It's a long way to Tipperary,
> and the sweetest girl I know.'

HOME AGAIN

It was a wonderful feeling to get safely back to Locre that evening, knowing that the next day I would be on my way home. Early in the morning I passed through Bailleul, which was being bombed at the time, and by evening was in Boulogne, dining sumptuously. I was in even higher spirits the next morning as I boarded the leave-boat and crossed the Channel, with a naval escort. It was a stirring sight to see the White Cliffs of Dover; there was England, the buttress of freedom, defiant and unconquerable.

The fast journey to Victoria in a luxurious Pullman was like a dream. The excellence of the meal added to the pleasure and the sense of growing excitement at the prospect of seeing May, my parents and home again. I found myself marvelling at the orderly countryside through which we were passing, the absence of destruction or of devastated villages, not a ruined house to be seen.

Matthew arrived home in Dublin on 12th October. May was already there with his father and mother. May and he had a quiet and happy eight days together, visiting friends and relatives, going to the theatre and playing records. They had their photograph taken, wedding rings well displayed. Matthew's brother, Austin, who had been wounded in France, happened to come home at the same time. His father wrote on the day Matthew left 'We all saw dear Matthew off to France and the trenches. Noble boy, I feel so proud of him, so gentle and so brave. God bless and protect him.'

BACK IN THE LINE

I was back in France, this time in a hotel in Calais, where I spent the night. I thought how quickly the ten days of my leave had sped, my feelings now were in sharp contrast to the romance of the home-coming. After a tiring journey I arrived back in Locre. At the quarter master's stores I came face to face with a newly painted cross bearing the name of a good friend, whom I had last seen, merry and well, just before I went on leave. He had been sniped through the heart while in charge of a wiring party at the 'Glory Hole'.

I reached the front line before midnight. Cheerful faces greeted me in the little dugout and I was given my share of the rum-punch. We were wonderful comrades, a common cause bound us together in a fellowship which gave each of us strength.

THE STOKES GUN

By this stage in the war the British had made great strides in trench mortar development. The new Stokes Gun was coming out in large numbers and many were being fitted up in the front line. The gunner sat with a 'stove-pipe' between his knees, its base resting on a mounting, into the barrel of which he placed a long cylindrical bomb with a cartridge at one end. On pulling a lanyard the bomb fell to the bottom where the charge was ignited and shot the projectile high into the air. It made a mighty crash on impact and must have caused exasperation to our 'friends' opposite.

It now became the custom for us to carry out systematic trench mortar strafes. Everything would be got ready beforehand, several hundred bombs collected, fused, charged, and placed beside each gun. Half the company would then go to the support line to avoid excessive casualties when the inevitable enemy retaliation came. The rest would thin out along the trench. At a prearranged signal twenty or so mortars would fire rapidly, sometimes for as long as an hour, over a narrow front, sending showers of bombs into the air in a constant stream. Seconds later deafening explosions would occur and the enemy's line would look as though it had been blown completely into the air. On one occasion I saw an enemy soldier lifted clean out of his trench. The German response would then come, with bigger trench mortar bombs than ours but at a slower rate of fire, encouraging us to keep up our bombardment and enabling us usually to get the better of the exchanges.

One morning nearly all our breastworks were blown in by

enemy mortars. For half-an-hour we had a bad time dodging around traverses in the trench. In one instance the place where a few of us had been standing was blown to bits a few seconds after we had run from it. With eyes fixed on the sky we were chased up and down the trench as bombs came from several directions. The only chance was to remain cool and not move until the last moment. All the time the noise from our mortars, retaliating as fast as they could, was deafening, but comforting.

A MOMENT OF NUMBNESS

An inexplicable thing happened to me one day. The trench had been partially demolished, the ground immediately in front and in rear of where we were standing had been struck by bombs. We looked up and sighted a bomb soaring up into the air above us. The soldiers around me ran out wildly into the open. For the first time I seemed suddenly to lose the will to live. I felt it was no use fighting against fate, that if I were to be killed it would be better to die quickly and without panic.

I remained sitting alone in the trench on the fire-step and watched the large black bomb as it turned in its flight and came spinning down towards me. I was confident that my end would be instantaneous. It must have been a further four or five seconds before the bomb struck, to me it seemed much longer. It missed the trench by inches and grazed the remains of the badly damaged sandbag wall immediately behind me. Either a slight deflection by the wind or a minor change in the mortar's elevation may have saved my life.

The instinct of self-preservation was quick to return; I flung myself flat in the trench. A moment later, stunned by the proximity of the explosion, covered with clay and bits of sandbag, I sprang up and ran like a hare towards the men, who welcomed me back as one from the dead.

On another occasion I was in charge of a working party at night, draining the ground some distance behind the front line. The water was about two feet deep and underneath was a sediment of thick sticky mud of the type which made life in Flanders unbearable. The men wore thigh gumboots and were working in water which came up above their knees. It had been quiet for a time when suddenly I spotted six streaks of sparks rising from the enemy's line, their arcs concentrating unmistakably on our position. I shouted to the men, who looked up and saw the approaching bombs. Their boots were wedged in the mud, whereupon they leapt out of them as one man and ran for cover in their stockinged feet. In a few seconds six large mortar bombs exploded exactly where they had been working. Barely a trace of the gumboots remained.

Once when taking over an active part of the line we found the remains of a leg with a boot on it protruding from a mound. It became the custom for anyone passing to give the boot a hurried polish with his sleeve. In another place it was an arm that was exposed, which no one passed without according it a handshake. The British soldier's sense of humour seldom deserted him and I marvelled at how he adapted it to the circumstances. It was not out of callousness or disrespect, we knew that it might be our hand or boot next, but we had to find a way of contending with the conditions under which we lived and not be suppressed by them.

NIGHT PATROLS

Each night an officer took out a patrol of three or four men and crawled about in no-man's-land. The purpose was usually to observe the condition of the enemy's wire or to ensure he was not concentrating a raiding party in front of his trenches to surprise us. Our patrols had to move cautiously to avoid being seen or heard and took care to avoid running unexpectedly into an enemy patrol sent out for the same purpose. Once, when it was almost dawn, a member of my patrol was killed alongside the enemy wire. Knowing we had been spotted it was useless to try and retrieve him in order to bring him back. It meant waiting until the following night before returning to recover him.

The long grass and water-logged shell holes meant we were usually wringing-wet on return from a patrol. After a stiff tot of rum we were soon asleep, to be woken up a few hours later to go on 2 or 3 hours watch, apparently none the worse for the soaking.

We too had to keep on the lookout for enemy patrols or raiding parties by night. We usually mounted four or five sentry groups in the company line, two men from each group on duty at one time while the others tried to get some sleep in a small shelter alongside. The officer-on-watch would walk up and down spending a few minutes in turn with each sentry, standing beside him on the fire-step, peering into the unknown. If there were reason to suspect enemy movement in front he would fire a Very light and have a look. This would continue throughout the night against a background of intermittent machine-gun bursts as both sides sprayed the trenches opposite them. Sometimes one of our sentries would be hit by a stray bullet, but that seldom occurred if he were alert and careful.

When I was officer-on-watch one evening a patrol returned and reported that the enemy were forming up in no-man's-land. They had counted about 50 of them climbing out of the trench and lining up in front of their wire. I ran along the line ordering all men to stand-to and alerted Company Headquarters. Our trench mortar officer, who at the time was in a dugout having a mug of tea, responded with great speed and in no time got his six mortars into action. In the meantime I phoned our artillery for support. Every rifle and machine-gun was now firing, backed up by salvos of trench mortar bombs which hurtled across and burst on the enemy's wire.

In the fading light we could just see the dark figures of the enemy fleeing before our murderous fire and trying to regain their trench. At the same time the first salvo of six shells from our artillery whistled overhead and burst in the midst of the enemy infantry. I had never before heard such rapid rifle fire and I suspect few of the enemy could have got back to their line safely. Our men cheered loudly. The Germans were undoubtedly on the point of raiding us as within a few moments a box-barrage was put down all around our trench, suggesting that their artillery was not aware of the fate of their raiding party and were keeping to their plan of isolating our stretch of trench. The vigilance of our patrol had resulted in the enemy party being almost completely wiped out before it had even started on its intended raid.

An artillery duel now took place and for several hours they gave us a bad time. Eventually our 'heavies' responded to our urgent telephone requests and as we now had superiority in guns we usually had the last word, as we did on this occasion; the enemy relapsed into silence.

RECREATION

On Boxing Day, 1916, we were resting in 'Kemmel Shelters', in the lee of the hill, which consisted of a small camp of wooden huts on the road to Kemmel, several miles behind the line. We were having a day off and I was watching the men playing football. Suddenly we heard the unmistakable whistle of shells in the air, followed by several bursts beside the goal post. Six of our men were killed or wounded. We buried three of them that night in the old cemetery beside the ruined church in Kemmel.

At about this time we bought a gramophone for our Company Mess and every now and then we got records from home. It was a great boon and prompted fellows from other companies to visit us and listen to the music. We would sit around our deal table in the hut at night, lighted candles stuck in bottles, drinking our whisky-sodas, waxing lyrical over a recent song or the latest two-step. One newly joined and over-enthusiastic subaltern drew showers of abuse one cold evening for his choice of *When you come to the end of a perfect day*!

The winter was long and intensely cold, causing many cases of frostbite. It must have been the supply of spirits which kept most of us alive. After a thaw the trenches used to tumble in, which, added to enemy bombardment, made them in places almost untenable. When we were in the support line I had sometimes to go up to the front during the night with a party, carrying picks and shovels, to help repair the trench before daylight. This sometimes meant digging out men who had been buried or partially buried, some still alive.

THE SNIPER

We had been several months in the Kemmel sector and were becoming active in trench mortaring, raiding, shelling and straffing. These operations inevitably prompted a reaction from the Germans making it more and more difficult for us to maintain our breastworks in a good state of repair and to keep the trench habitable. Sniping by both sides had greatly increased, we walked warily by day knowing that to expose the top few inches of one's head would instantly draw a bullet. On one occasion a recently joined soldier bobbed his head up and down, during which a bullet grazed the top of his helmet. With a look of indignant surprise he confided to me 'dem fellers would shoot yer' – an unarguable, if hardly a penetrating, deduction.

It was difficult to restrain the men's curiosity, sometimes in a momentary lapse they would peep over the top during daylight. The crack of a bullet would follow, a body would collapse on the duckboard with blood flowing from the forehead, two stretcher bearers would be summoned; and the war went on.

We too had snipers and there was a post in the support line on high ground overlooking parts of the enemy trench not visible from our forward position. I visited them one morning and watched the Corporal in charge – well known to our battalion as a first-class shot. His companion had his eyes glued to a telescope while he kept himself almost fully concealed behind an artificial mound.

These men showed great patience and they waited quietly for an hour or so before the observer indicated he could see his target. I looked through a telescope and saw a large steel helmet and unshaven face of a German rise up slowly to peer

2/Lieut Matthew Cooper, just commissioned: April 1915.

May and Matthew, first leave from France: October 1916.

Scottish Regiment keeping watch with periscopes: 1915.

Ruins of Loos, cellars of houses were used as dugouts: 1915.

Mine shaft entrance. Sappers working below, short of air, did not welcome its use by other troops as a refuge from shelling.

A slag heap at Philosophe, typical of the coal-mining country around Loos, in use as an observation post: 1915.

The railway line at Philosophe, as it is today, where Matthew 'froze' while marching his platoon across; miraculously all escaped injury.

'The road that ran from Kemmel Town'.

Spanbroekmolen mine crater four days after the explosion, Battle of Messines: June 1917.

Spanbroekmolen crater, now 'Pool of Peace', in 1931, looking back towards the British line, which once ran through the battered ground beyond the rim. Kemmel hill and town in background.

Ulster Division on Messines Ridge after highly succesful attack: 7 June 1917.

One of many German pillboxes on Messines Ridge blown up at start of the battle: June 1917.

Life as usual in the Officers Mess on Messines Ridge: June 1917.

'Pool of Peace' today, shrunk from the huge Spanbroekmolen crater of June 1917.

Royal Inniskilling Fusiliers with trophies after Battle of Messines: June 1917.

Nuns with their young wards at Major Redmond's grave at Locre Hospice in September 1917; badly wounded on the first day of the Battle of Messines he died shortly afterwards in their care.

In the flat country behind Ypres, German artillery observation balloons made the roads highly dangerous.

Large Howitzer at 'Salvation Corner', Ypres.

One of the small bunkers occupied by Matthew's platoon still stands today in a pasture on the edge of Wieltje.

Canal bank at Ypres a short distance behind the front where Matthew and his men found 'comparative peace': 1917.

Matthew nearly came to grief when crossing one of these bridges over the canal at Ypres by night.

Ypres Cloth Hall and Belfry, Cathedral in background, before the War.

'The jagged finger of the Cloth Hall', Ypres: 1918.

Main Street, Ypres; ruins of Cloth Hall in background: 1916.

Totally destroyed by 1918, Ypres Cloth Hall and Belfry and Cathedral were rebuilt afterwards to their original design.

Locre Hospice, once the scene of happy memories, levelled to the ground and in German hands: April 1918.

Anglo-Belgian-New Zealand Remembrance Service on 75th anniversary of the Battle, held at Messines Ridge British Cemetery: 6th June 1992.

over his trench. The Corporal put on a green mask to avoid being detected, leant over the trench in the long grass, took aim through the telescopic sights fitted to his rifle, and fired. But he was a fraction too late, our cautious quarry had ducked down behind the sandbags just in time, the bullet probably grazing the top of his tin hat. To our amusement the German raised his arm and hastily described several circles, the recognised practice range signal for a 'miss'! Rather a sport – that Hun – I thought, but he didn't try it a second time.

The Corporal told me that a relief was due in half-an-hour, so we waited and watched. It must have been more like an hour before another head slowly emerged from the sandbags. The Corporal fired. There was no 'miss signal' this time, a few minutes later two stretcher-bearers made their way along the German trench. The enemy's strength on the Western Front had been reduced by one.

PREPARATION FOR BATTLE

Most of the time we were now holding the front either in the region of Spanbroekmolen or Vierstraat and when in reserve were back in Locre. Our tactical position was inferior to that of the enemy as they occupied the higher ground along the Messines Ridge from where they overlooked our trenches and the roads behind. In the early spring a strong rumour was circulating that we would be launching a major battle to capture the Ridge. Preparations soon began and we found that instead of resting when out of the line we were working almost continuously on heavy and laborious duties. Miles of new trenches had to be dug in which to assemble attacking troops.

Literally hundreds of new gun pits and emplacements were prepared for the expected influx of new artillery units. A network of light railway tracks was laid together with some large-gauge lines. All of this had to be concealed from the enemy which meant working under cover of darkness and using camouflage.

It was now April and our brigade was ordered out of the line to a training area near St Omer, a total march of 50 miles, during which we covered about 15 miles a day. It was a welcome change to leave the trenches and find ourselves marching through peaceful countryside and quiet villages. We set off early each morning and in the evenings were billeted in small townships on the way. It was encouraging to have so few 'fallers-out', considering that much of the battalion was composed of fresh drafts from home. We remained in our new location for a week, training hard, starting at platoon level, then company, ending on the last day with a brigade assault on a ridge similar to Messines, on which a replica of the enemy trench system had been marked out with tapes. Our signallers were instructed on the new procedure for keeping in touch with a 'contact aeroplane'. The signs were unmistakable, this was a dress rehearsal for a big attack at Messines.

We marched back to Locre over the next three days in unusually warm weather for early spring. There we found more and more preparations under way with new camps being set up to accommodate extra troops. When not in the line we continued to work hard at night, starting at dusk and continuing until dawn, digging trenches and preparing for the arrival of new troops. We disliked these working parties as the enemy knew there was something in the air and every night we had to run the gauntlet of fire on the roads behind the line. The first red streak of morning was a welcome sight with the prospect of breakfast and some sleep.

One of our jobs was to lay telephone lines linking companies to one another and to headquarters, extending back several miles behind the line. This meant digging narrow cable ducts 4 to 5 feet deep. One night we were engaged in cable-laying from the front line to the support trench, 'Watling Street'. While we were working, our troops launched a raid on the enemy lines directly in front of us.

In a few moments the enemy replied with large calibre shells, choosing as his target the place where we were digging. As the first salvo burst around us we ran for the nearest trench. The shells were coming down so close that the men started to run about wildly, along the trench and out in the open. Lives can be lost in this sort of confusion and panic, so I deliberately calmed myself, called to the men to remain in the trench and to sit tight.

I settled down myself at the bottom of the trench and this had the desired effect of encouraging several of the men to join me. A moment later there was a deafening burst beside us and several of the men who were with me again dashed off. Yet another shell burst further down the trench in the direction they were running, so back they raced and we all remained huddled together in the dark. For nearly an hour we sat in this open trench, in which there were no dugouts, while all the time large shells shrieked through the air, several rounds falling each minute, bursting with nerve-shattering force on each side, covering us with clay and gravel. The trench was about 4 feet wide at the top, with no breastworks, but the shells falling on each side somehow just missed the open top.

A boy beside me, who had left his home only a few months before, started to weep as a shell fell even closer, stunning us by its explosion. I found it helped me to keep my own self-control trying to settle him and cheer his spirits. I had become utterly fatalistic, resigned to death and thinking that it would not be so bad so long as I were not alone at the time and it were instantaneous. At last the bombardment stopped for the night and at dawn we were able to see that the trench had been almost demolished. On both sides of where we had been crouching were two large pits, spattered with churned-up clay and debris, in which shell after shell had fallen.

Throughout this period when we were preparing for the coming battle enemy artillery continued at night to make life dangerous and unpleasant for us, concentrating their shelling on the roads which our transports used for bringing up rations. This led the Army Commander to issue an order that every gun on the 2nd Army front would put down 5 minutes rapid fire at 7 o'clock one evening in retaliation. When the time came I was leading a working party up to the trenches and we heard the sound of hundreds of our guns bursting forth. I got my men quickly into a trench to wait for the inevitable enemy reply before continuing on. Then it came, causing us no casualties, though shells whined overhead in both directions, many crashing into a wood close by. The Commander's plan was that if the enemy put down a counter-bombardment we would start up again at 9 o'clock, this time for ten minutes. At that hour all hell broke loose, allowing us a superb view of the blaze of bursting shells falling on the long Messines Ridge.

After ten minutes our guns stopped, but not so the enemy's, whereupon our barrage resumed for another ten minutes. This had the desired effect and the Boche did not fire another gun that night on our front. Our shell superiority was now beginning to tell and for some time after that exchange our transports were left alone.

One night we had finished handing over the line to another battalion and were in nearby dugouts getting ready to march to Locre when the enemy sent out a large raiding party under cover of a heavy bombardment. We saw the SOS rocket signals going up from our line and were immediately ordered to man a disused trench behind the support line. It was perilous getting to it over several open fields through the shell bursts. We raced across in small parties and on reaching the trench set up our Lewis guns, ready to give the Hun a warm reception. To our disappointment he didn't come. We heard afterwards his raiding party had been driven back with considerable loss and failed even to reach our front line. The battalion in the line which had just taken over from us suffered heavily from the enemy bombardment.

At that time of the year the weather was good and in the evening, when in reserve at 'Kemmel Shelters', the men would visit Kemmel YMCA, and the officers not on duty would sit around the mess table in candlelight. One evening we were playing bridge when we were disturbed unexpectedly by shells falling on our camp, something that hadn't happened before. Fortunately only one man was wounded, despite a direct hit on a hut normally occupied by twenty. We got the men out of the camp quickly and returned when the shelling had stopped. The following evening we were sentimentalising over the beauty of the night and the music from the gramophone, enjoying our comradeship, when the shelling started again. We resented this interruption to our rest period in reserve and the discomfort it was causing us, especially as this time there had been some casualties. The next night we moved to a nearby wood where we were able to sleep in peace.

It was now evident that the day of the long-awaited battle was drawing near. Under cover of darkness, guns and howitzers of all sizes rumbled along the roads towards the front. The convoys seemed endless, six or eight horses pulling the smaller guns, large traction engines trailed the mighty 8″ and 9.2″ weapons. On reaching their allotted positions the guns were carefully hidden and camouflaged. These batteries became known as 'The Circus' because they moved about the long front giving 'performances' so as to confuse the enemy as to our intentions and as to the exact battle positions they would later occupy.

PRE-BATTLE RAID

The battalion was now ordered to carry out a large scale raid with 4 officers and 200 men on the night of the 5th June. There was much competition among the officers to be selected. I was one of the ones with the longest war service and my claim to take part was upheld. A length of enemy trench about 500 yards was chosen and aeroplane photos taken of it. We selected a piece of ground to the rear similar to the enemy's position and marked out their trenches on it, with tapes, to conform to the photograph, and carried out a number of practice raids.

The raiding party was divided into two waves, single lines about 30 yards apart, whose task was to clear the enemy from their first and second line trenches. They were to be accompanied by small supporting parties having specific tasks, such as blocking off escape from the ends of the trench being raided, mopping up inside the captured trenches, protecting our flanks with Lewis guns, and rounding up prisoners. Machine-guns would isolate the area under attack by firing on a wide semicircle around the back of the enemy trenches. For several days we practised our parts over the tapes. I could not help contrasting the small restricted night raids we used to carry out in the Loos sector, when I arrived there in 1916, with the large scale, carefully organised, ambitious raids we now mounted.

Those of us who were part of the raiding party were relieved from routine duty the night before and slept in dugouts. That same night a party went out to cut gaps in our own wire.

The original Operation Order for this raid is reproduced in this section. It gives the detailed plan, describing the objectives and the functions of the various groups involved, including Matthew Cooper's command of the platoon to capture the northern part of the German front line and the use of runners and signalling lamps to report progress. The trenches in the German defence system had been given names, e.g. Nail Switch, Support Row, Nag Support, which were printed on the current Ordnance Survey maps.

On the day of the raid bombs and ammunition were issued to those taking part and their identification badges and letters collected from them. During daylight our artillery shelled the enemy wire to cut gaps. Before dusk the members of our raiding party were interspersed with the troops holding our front immediately opposite the enemy line to be raided. We got ready as quietly as we could. Shortly before Zero I passed along the trench and gave final instructions to the men as they stood, tense and grim, with a bright nervous glint in their eyes, understandably feeling the strain of waiting. Theirs was the expression of men ready to do what was expected of them.

I decided to use a narrow ditch which ran immediately in front of us in no-man's-land as a jumping off ground. If the enemy should gain the slightest inkling that a raid on their lines was imminent the result could be disastrous – the loss of most of our party through machine-gun fire. It was a clear evening in early June, not fully dark, which meant we had to take great care in getting into the ditch to avoid giving anything away. Silently, in twos and threes, we slid over the parapet and wriggled forward into the hollow. A few minutes later we were all in position, 'like greyhounds on the leash', waiting for 10 pm.

When the hour came the air was rent with the crash of guns and the shrieking of hundreds of projectiles over our heads. The German trench in front of us was engulfed in a long line of bursting shells and clouds of smoke. Simultaneously our trench mortars coughed out their deadly missiles, machine-guns pounded streams of bullets into the enemy lines. We sprang from the ditch and raced across no-man's-land, tripping over barbed-wire and stumbling into water-logged shell holes. We were stunned by the enormity of our own fire and became oblivious to all except the urge to go forward.

When the first frantic rush was over we were forced to pause near the enemy trench while the terrifying bombardment from our 18-pounder guns and 4.5″ howitzers continued. The barrage did not lift and move forward as I had expected, instead shells continued to fall in front of us. For one dreadful moment, as in a dream, I thought that something catastrophic had gone wrong with the artillery fireplan or an unforeseen occurrence had thrown our arrangements into disorder. Then I remembered, the operation order stated that our artillery would maintain their fire on the enemy's front line for two minutes. In our eagerness we had rushed across no-man's-land in much less time.

Soon our barrage lifted on to their second line and we were able quickly to pass through the tattered remains of the enemy's wire and leap into their badly damaged front line trench. Many of the enemy had been killed in the bombardment and the survivors fled when they saw us coming. Some were bayonetted but most of them ran back only to find themselves caught once more in the barrage, now falling on their second line, and there they perished. Meanwhile the mopping-up parties ran along the communication trenches throwing bombs into their dugouts.

ORDERS FOR RAID. SECRET.

Reference Map OOSTTAVERNE Part of Sheet 28. 1/5000

1. A raid will be carried out by the 8th. Battalion R. Inniskilling Fusiliers on the night of 5/6th. June 1917. Zero Hour will be 10 p.m.

2. Raiding Party will be drawn from "A" & "C" Coys. 8th. R. Innis. Fus. and will consist of 4 Officers and approximately 170 Men.
O.C. Enterprise Capt. C.H. Godsland M.C.

3. RAID AREA.
Northern Boundary N.18.b.20.28 – N.18.b.60.15.
Southern Boundary N.18.d.14.70 – N.18.d.50.75.
Eastern Boundary N.18.b.60.15 – N.18.d.50.75.

4. OBJECT. To damage enemy personnel, works, &c., to capture prisoners and to obtain information regarding the state of the enemy trenches

5. OBJECTIVES. 1st. Objective German Front Line.
2nd. Objective NAIL SWITCH.

METHOD OF ATTACK. The raiding party will attack in 2 waves, the first wave consisting of "C" Coy. will take the first objective, the second wave consisting of "A" Coy. will take the second objective. distance between waves will be 30 yards and each wave will consist of 1 line.

1st Objective. O.C. "C" Coy. will arrange to provide the following parties.

(1) 3 Blocking Parties consisting of 1 N.C.O. and 4 men each to block the following points, N.18.b.20.28, N.18.d.20.78, N.18.d.14.70.
(2) A Mopping Up Party of 1 N.C.O. and 8 for NAG ROW.
(3) A Mopping Up Party of 1 N.C.O. and 8 who will work in a Northerly direction along SUPPORT ROW.
(4) A Left Flank Party of 1 N.C.O. and 4 along Northern Raid Boundary.
(5) Two Lewis Guns alongBECK at N.18.b.12.32.
(6) A Right Flank Party of 1 N.C.O. and 4 along Boundary between Support Line and NAIL SWITCH.
(7) Two Lewis Guns along BECK at N.18.d.05.75.
(8) A Prisoner Collecting Station of 1 N.C.O. and 4 Men near Sap at N.18. Central.

2/Lieut. Cooper will be responsible for the Northern Part of 1st. Objective to N.18.d.20.95.

2/Lieut. Robbins will be responsible for the Southern Part of 1st. Objective.

Second Objective. O.C. "A" Coy. will arrange to provide the following parties.

(1) Blocking Party for North end of NAIL SWITCH of 1 N.C.O. and 8 Men.
(2) Blocking Party for South end of NAIL SWITCH of 1 N.C.O and 4 Men.
(3) Right Flank Party posted about N.18.d.60.75 and consisting of 1 Lewis Gun and 1 N.C.O. and 4 Men.
(4) A Prisoner Collecting Station of 1 N.C.O. and 4 Men at N.18.d.60.90.

Capt. Hornby will be responsible for the 2nd. Objective and will have with him 2/Lieut. Notley.

All Lewis Gun Teams will consist of 2 Men each, extra magazines being carried up by Assaulting Troops and dumped.

ACTION OF ARTILLERY. See Appendix "A"

ACTION OF STOKES MORTARS.
To commence at Zero and continue until all raiding party are back
(1) To fire on SUNKEN ROAD from N.18.b 22.52 to N.18.b.70.28.
(2) N.18.d.24.58 – N.18.d.20.20.

9. ACTION OF MACHINE GUNS.
To commence at Zero and continue until all Raiding Party are back M.G. SUPPORT to SUNKEN ROAD, CHATEAU SPUR, UNNAMED WOOD, BLACK COT, Southern End of NAIL SWITCH from N.18.d.50.55. - N.18.d.40.30.

10. WITHDRAWAL.
(1) When the parties under Capt. Hornby, 2/Lieuts. Cooper and Robbins have completed their task, these Officers will send back 3 runners each to O.C. Enterprise to report completion of task. Battalion Signal Officer will detail 2 Signallers to report to Capt. Hornby with Lucas Signalling Lamp. The signal on lamp that task is completed will be a succession of dashes.
(2) Recall Signal will consist of Golden Rain Rockets fired in quick succession from front line.

(3) "C" Coy. will not withdraw until "A" Coy. have passed through them.
(4) The Lewis Guns of "C" Coy. will cover the withdrawal of "C" Coy.
(5) B.L.G.O. will arrange Lewis Guns in our Front Line to cover withdrawal.

11. H.Q. of O.C. Enterprise will be at BYRON FARM which is in direct communication with Brigade H.Q.
Watches will be synchronised at Battn. H.Q. (S.P. 13) at Zero minus 6 hours and minus 2 hours.
O.C. Enterprise will arrange to have sufficient Orderlies with him to be able to send messages forward.

12. The M.O. will arrange to have an Advanced Dressing Station near BYRON FARM. The Stretcher Bearers of "A" & "C" Coys. will not go over with their Coys. but will be under the orders of the M.O.

13. DISTINGUISHING MARKS. "A" Coy. will wear Yellow Arm Bands, "C" Coy. will wear no Arm Bands.

14. Probable Duration of Raid, 1 Hour.

15. EQUIPMENT. All ranks will be lightly equipped carrying rifle and bayonet and two bombs in pocket. Special Bombing Parties will be provided with Bombing Waistcoats.

16. O.C. Enterprise will take steps to see that no one taking part in the raid has any maps, papers &c., in his possession.

17. All papers and other articles that may be of use for purposes identification must be removed from dead Germans and brought back.

18. Prisoners and all articles brought from enemy lines must be sent direct to Battn. H.Q.

Lieut. Colonel.,
Commanding.....,
8th. R. Inniskilling Fusiliers...

3 / 6 / 17.

The second attacking wave now arrived, commanded by Jumbo Hornby, and as soon as our guns lifted their fire onto the next objective they went forward to attack the enemy's second line. As expected, we now heard distant booms from behind the enemy lines and soon shells were falling all around us, thickened up by heavy trench mortar bombs fired from the ridge in front. Several of my men were wounded and taken back to our own line. I sent word by runner to the 'Officer Commanding Enterprise' that we had completed our part of the raid and were now giving support to Jumbo in his attack on the enemy's second line. Shortly afterwards a large rocket soared up from behind us breaking into a shower of coloured stars, the prearranged signal for us to withdraw.

My task now was to cover the withdrawal of the whole raiding party. I moved to the left flank with my team of two Lewis guns to guard against a possible counter-attack and remained there until the raiding party had returned through our position. Shells were continuing to fall and it was difficult to make oneself heard in the din. I rather prided myself that I had been smoking a cigarette from the time we reached the German line!

When the raiding party had all returned to our line, following the recall signal, Jumbo Hornby was missing. We sent a search party back to the enemy lines to look for him. They found him, badly wounded, and brought him back. We called the roll to account for everyone before sending word back to our gunners to stop the barrage. Our casualties were 1 officer and 13 other ranks wounded. Nine prisoners had been captured and were told to make their own way rearwards, but they had to cross no-man's-land under heavy fire and only four reached our lines.

When morning came our battalion left the front and marched back to 'Doncaster Huts' in Locre, tired but well satisfied.

Matthew received a special citation from Major-General Hickie, Commander 16th Division, for his part in the raid and his 'name and deed' were entered in the Record of the

16th Division.

THE BATTLE OF MESSINES

The following evening we were told to put on battle equipment, issued with special rations, and ordered to return to the line. We were certain now that the long-awaited major offensive for which we had prepared so thoroughly was about to begin. Before parading I went to the little shed in Locre which served as an Officers' Club and found it crowded with others from our division. There we drank to the success of the coming battle, realising that for some of us it would be the last. I saw Major Willie Redmond there, of the 6th Battalion Royal Irish Fusiliers, who was killed the next day and buried by the Nuns close to Locre Hospice. He was the younger brother of John Redmond, the famous Irish Parliamentary leader.

Redmond was wounded on the first day of the Battle of Messines, in the leading wave of the attack, and was taken to the Hospice where he was nursed by the Nuns. He died the same day, at the age of 56, and was buried in the Hospice grounds. His grave can easily be found, close to the Locre Hospice Military Cemetery, where it stands alone, where he was first laid to rest. Nearby stands an imposing hostel, built after the war, where to this day Nuns look after orphaned and abandoned children.

We marched at 10 pm to the assembly area in absolute silence, no smoking, bayonets as yet unfixed lest the enemy should see them flash in the moonlight or other illumination. We saw silent columns of men moving towards the front across fields, on every track, on every road. Wherever we looked there were guns, their grim and reassuring outlines partly concealed in hedges and copses, silently waiting. At midnight we were back at the front, in position, in a newly-dug trench, while everywhere around crowded ranks of men lay sleeping or waiting.

An issue of rum arrived at 1 am and with it the message that the mines would go up at 3.07 am with Zero three minutes later. We had heard so much about these mines, that digging had started a year and a half ago and the amount of explosive in some of the galleries exceeded anything that had ever been used before. Less convincing was the brief that if any mine had not gone up by Zero-plus-15 seconds we could advance on the safe assumption that it would not detonate at all!

The secrecy surrounding the mobilisation of troops and weapons for the offensive, and the care taken to ensure absolute silence in the trenches that night, must have been effective. The enemy did not seem to be aware of what was taking place. Had there been an enemy bombardment on our forward positions at the moment when all our attacking troops were in their starting positions, the result could have spelled disaster. Shells bursting in these crowded trenches would have caused horrifying casualties. After midnight, as customary, the enemy shelled the roads and tracks well to the rear, but by then they were empty, the silent army had already moved through. We drank our issue of rum and tried to sleep in the bottom of the trench. At 2 am I awoke coughing and choking, poison gas was drifting back in the gentle wind from our gun positions in the rear, on which we could hear enemy shells falling. I ordered respirators to be worn and we tried to get back to sleep.

Shortly before 3 am I stood on the fire-step and looked out. The first glow of dawn was discernible. Some desultory shelling was taking place and a few Very lights were twinkling, looking pale against the sky with the onset of daylight. In that comparative peace there was no harbinger to warn of the convulsion that in a few minutes would be unleashed in front of us.

Exactly at 3.07 am the earth trembled and shook. Men lying on the fire-step tumbled into the trench. Shock waves passed through the ground causing trenches to collapse. I clung to the parapet as I watched a huge dense column of flame rise slowly from a part of the Messines Ridge immediately in front of me, surrounded by clouds of black smoke, dust and debris. I was awe-struck and fascinated. Almost immediately there was a thunderous explosion, sustained for what seemed like half a minute. The fiery pillar rose several hundred feet in the air, became enveloped in a pall of smoke, then faded into blackness, leaving the ground to continue its violent shaking.

Along the extensive battle front simultaneous explosions were occurring, adding to the tumultuous commotion, and reverberations. One of the mines, close to us on our right, towards Spanbroekmolen, seemed to be the largest. It had completely demolished a massive concrete strong-point containing machine-gun emplacements and dugouts manned by a company of the enemy; none could have survived. The shock was devastating, so much so that one of the men close to me fell down shivering and babbling and had to be led away.

Nineteen mines in all exploded along the Messines Ridge that early morning, several of them in front of where Matthew was waiting. The 'Spanbroekmolen' mine was detonated over 1000 yards to the right of him and although others exploded nearer to where he was standing, it was the biggest and is almost certainly the one to which he refers.

The mine had a crater diameter of 430 feet, a depth below ground level of 40 feet, and a rim width of 90 feet. The charge consisted of 91,000 lbs of ammonal laid at a depth of 88 feet below the surface. The pit was known afterwards by British troops as the 'Lone Tree Crater', the name given later also to the nearby military cemetery. The remains of the crater are preserved to this day, as a memorial, filled with water, fish and lilies, rechristened 'The Pool of Peace'. Other craters can be found on the Ridge.

The advice given to the troops that 'if a mine has not detonated within 15 seconds of Zero Hour it can be assumed that it will not explode at all' would seem in retrospect to have been an expediency, necessary for the success of the attack as a whole. A hundred yards or so from the rim of the crater, in Lone Tree Cemetery, lie the graves of men of the Royal Irish Rifles who tragically left their trench too early and were caught in the explosion of their own mine at Spanbroekmolen. An unexploded mine from that same battle went up on its own in July 1955 but fortunately caused little damage!

As the cloud of smoke cleared an awesome hush descended over the battlefield for a few moments, as though the earth itself was stunned by so vast an upheaval. Showers of German multi-coloured SOS signals were appearing in the sky, but nothing could help them now. Like a succession of thunder-claps, hundreds and hundreds of our guns opened fire behind us, thousands of shells screamed overhead. In an instant the whole Messines Ridge was blotted out by a dense screen of smoke and dust. Simultaneously we heard the continuous cracking of bullets overhead as countless machine-guns behind us opened fire on the enemy lines. Mass formations of our fighting planes passed overhead using their machine-guns and bombs to add to the havoc behind the enemy lines.

The start of our artillery barrage was the signal for a long line of khaki figures to emerge quickly from our trenches and form up in a number of separate lines in no-man's-land. The troops of the first wave were as steady as they would be on parade, barely three feet apart, their rifles at the high-port, their long sharp bayonets jutting out above their steel helmets. These men knew their business. Led by their officers at walking pace they went forward, soon to be swallowed up in the smoke and dust of the creeping barrage in front of them.

We were the second wave with orders to be ready to advance in half-an-hour. All around us the ground was spurting up as enemy guns replied, the deafening noise preventing us from hearing shells coming or even being aware of some of the bursts around us. One of my men was badly wounded. For half-an-hour we waited, unable to see what was happening, not knowing how the battle was going. Then we saw the first wounded returning, some walking, some on stretchers. These were followed by large groups of prisoners, all shapes and sizes, some in spectacles, most in ill-fitting dirty uniforms, some with bristled heads or close-cropped hair, others crowned with those ridiculous little peakless caps. They seemed scared, woebegone and hungry, many with a week's growth on their chin.

The battle orders to the 8th Battalion were that they were to follow the assault wave to help in 'mopping-up' the captured enemy trenches, and to carry key supplies needed to consolidate the ground gained and to enable the advance to continue. On reaching the first objective they were required to set up and mark these replenishment points at prearranged places and then return across the old no-man's-land to pick up further stores.

At last we were ordered forward and soon reached the newly captured ridge carrying our heavy loads of ammunition. We established supply dumps in the old German trenches as far forward as the Wytschaete-Vierstraat road, now a short distance behind our forward troops. We trudged back and forth over the battlefield carrying countless boxes of Mills bombs, small arms ammunition, signal cartridges, tins of water and other supplies and equipment, running the gauntlet of enemy long-range guns. I heard a cry of '*Wasser, Wasser*!' and catching sight of a wounded German soldier lying on the ground I went over to him and gave him a drink from my water-bottle. We used captured German prisoners to help bring up barbed wire. All day we toiled to and fro, performing a laborious task that did not have the dash of the assault wave, but was essential to the success of the attack.

The intensity of the fire we put down on the enemy helped to keep down our casualties. The arrangements for receiving the wounded were excellent, they were quickly taken away from the battlefield. We saw a number of our soldiers lying where they had fallen, facing the enemy, bayonets fixed, grasping their rifles firmly in both hands, as if determined still to continue their advance. For them the crusade was over, their duty to their country nobly done.

I watched with interest a tall hedge of young trees flatten as the grey nose of one of our tanks forced its way through, the vehicle lumbering awkwardly over the uneven ground.

Machine-guns poked out from slits at the front and a six-pounder barrel stuck out from each side. These vehicles sometimes dipped and wallowed in a trench, paused, then climbed out, slipping and rocking as they ploughed their way to the Ridge and beyond. Our orders stated that the tanks were there to support the infantry, who should never wait for them or gather around them.

Another corps had now come up to pass through the assault troops and continue the attack. It was midday before our barrage stopped, by which time light guns had trotted up and gone into action on positions which had previously been part of no-man's-land. I was watching a battery move forward when a large shell burst amongst them. I was sure that at least one of our guns and its team were 'goners', but they emerged from the smoke intact. We saw cavalry dismount on getting close to the enemy and go forward with their Hotchkiss guns.

Our corps had now achieved its task; fresh troops were being brought up to continue the attack beyond the Ridge. During one of the many journeys we made back to our old front line, to get ammunition, the company cook brought me a mess-tin of tea which looked more delicious than I can describe. As I raised it to my lips a shell exploded close by and blew it from my hands. Not long afterwards a large shell buried itself a few yards from me without exploding, prompting me to run fast, lest it should change its mind.

In the afternoon battalions of the fresh corps formed up on the newly won Messines Ridge and continued the advance. The tanks we had seen labour up the slope were in position to support the second phase of the battle. Our division gradually withdrew as these troops took over the offensive. We spent that night in a dugout which had been in our old front line before the attack and was now 4 or 5 miles behind our forward positions.

Our artillery, now firing from gun positions in front of us, were kept busy during the night responding to calls from our troops engaged in beating off counter-attacks. The casualties in our battalion were light. The joy of a great achievement was ours. The wearing of captured German caps, uniform or equipment was expressly forbidden in the orders for the battle but nearly everyone had collected booty of some sort. I too had collected some trophies from German prisoners, and asked our cook, who was about to go on leave, if he would deliver them to my home.

All the enemy force on a long battle front had been accounted for, thousands of prisoners and many guns had been captured. Over 400 prisoners had passed through our military police posts on their way back to brigade headquarters. To us it seemed that night had fallen on a day of great success and high drama, deserving a celebration. I had optimistically put a pack of cards in my haversack, so we sat down in the dugout to a rubber of bridge.

It was the view of many of us who took part in the Battle of Messines that it was the best planned and most successful battle on the Western Front. The mining of the Ridge which had taken so long to complete had been achieved under hazardous circumstances and was used to devastating effect. By noon on the first day the attacking troops had captured the enemy lines on a front of nearly 10 miles, outflanking the enemy positions at Ypres. We front line troops were confident and eager to push on to exploit this outstanding and unprecedented initial success, but we were ordered to dig in, in open country, and secure our new positions. The order astonished the victorious troops, allowing the enemy to rush up reinforcements and counter-attack the next day.

The British High Command saw Messines as necessary to secure the southern flank for the major battle to follow, afterwards known as Passchendaele. Exploitation of a possible breakthrough at the initial assault did not form part of their plan. The controversy over the decision not to exploit the success of the Messines attack continues to this day, especially in the light of the Passchendaele disaster.

The Battle of Messines is still commemorated by the Belgian people. On the 6th June 1992, the 75th anniversary of the battle, a remembrance service organised by the

Belgian authorities was held in the British cemetery in Messines attended by officials, organisations and visitors from Belgium, Britain and New Zealand, and as always, local people.

The German trophies which Matthew had asked the cook to deliver to his home were personally delivered two weeks after the battle, his father proudly noting in his diary that his son was clearly held in high esteem by the cook and the other men in his company.

AFTER MESSINES

Several days later we left the front and made a three day march to some small hamlets about 30 miles behind the line. We rested amid green fields and foliage, rich with the colours of June, where it was almost possible to forget the war; but not for long. We were soon sent nearer to the front and camped at Voormezele. Clearly we were on our way to Ypres where preparations were in hand for what must be another major attack. It would be no walkover as the enemy had learnt many lessons from the Battle of Messines and was concentrating his forces opposite Ypres.

As this was to be our division's first time in the Ypres Salient our company commanders and other officers were sent ahead to visit the line, to learn about the terrain and how best to lead their men into action. We set off one morning in a *chara-banc* along the road from Poperinge to Ypres, or 'Wipers' as it was known to the British Tommy, during which we witnessed a picture of desolation and destruction. We alighted from our transport near the ruins of this war-torn and legendary town and saw the jagged remains of the dominant Cloth Hall in the centre of what once had been the Belgian town of Ypres. Motor ambulances were making their way rearwards, testifying to the heavy casualties suffered in artillery bombardments. We had been waiting several hours for our guides close to where a dead horse and broken wagon lay in a field beside the road, when unexpectedly we received orders to cancel the visit and return to camp.

Half a mile down the road on the journey back we were hailed by a gunner who ran out from his emplacement shouting at the top of his voice for us to stop. Shells were falling on each side of the road so we did not much like the idea of stopping. When a moment later a salvo fell on the road just in front of us we were quick to comply. The gunner told us that transports were being hit every day along this stretch, coming as no surprise when at that moment we caught sight of an observation balloon above the German lines spotting for their artillery. It was a narrow escape. We waited a bit before continuing our journey back to camp, the *char-a-banc* crawling slowly over a road broken up by shell holes. No one spoke as we lumbered through the danger area until finally we were through, careering merrily along the road to Poperinge. My friend Jimmy sitting beside me swallowed a nip from his flask and passed it to me; no words were necessary.

It came as a surprise to me a few days later to be told I was due to go on leave, although it was nearly nine months since I had last been home. The news was most welcome as my health was not good, boils were again breaking out on my neck and head. My friends pulled my leg and said they did not like to see me leave for any reason as it usually meant that some big attack was imminent.

I was a happy man as I made the journey home, arriving in Dublin on 23rd July 1917, overjoyed at the thought of spending a few days with May and my parents and glad of the opportunity to be able to build up my health.

A few days later, on the 31st July 1917, the Third Battle of Ypres was launched (later known as 'Passchendaele'), in which the 8th Battalion suffered heavy casualties, losing nearly two thirds of their officers throughout the fighting. Shortly afterwards the two depleted sister battalions were amalgamated to form the 7/8th Royal Inniskilling Fusiliers.

The names of many Inniskilling Fusiliers who fought and fell in the Battle of Passchendaele or elsewhere in this part of Flanders, with no known grave, are inscribed on the memorial wall at Tyne Cot Military Cemetery. The cemetery is sited on the spot where some of the fiercest fighting took place during Passchendaele. Many others from the regiment who died in the Salient are commemorated on the Menin Gate at Ypres, with thousands and thousands of Commonwealth soldiers; or their names are to be found among the countless headstones in the tranquil and heart-moving military cemeteries which abound throughout this historic and unforgettable region.

Matthew was joined by May at his father's home. When the local Medical Officer saw the severity of his condition he sent him for treatment to the Military Hospital where he was detained, graded as unfit for immediate return to France.

PART 3 1918

'Wilderness of the Dead'

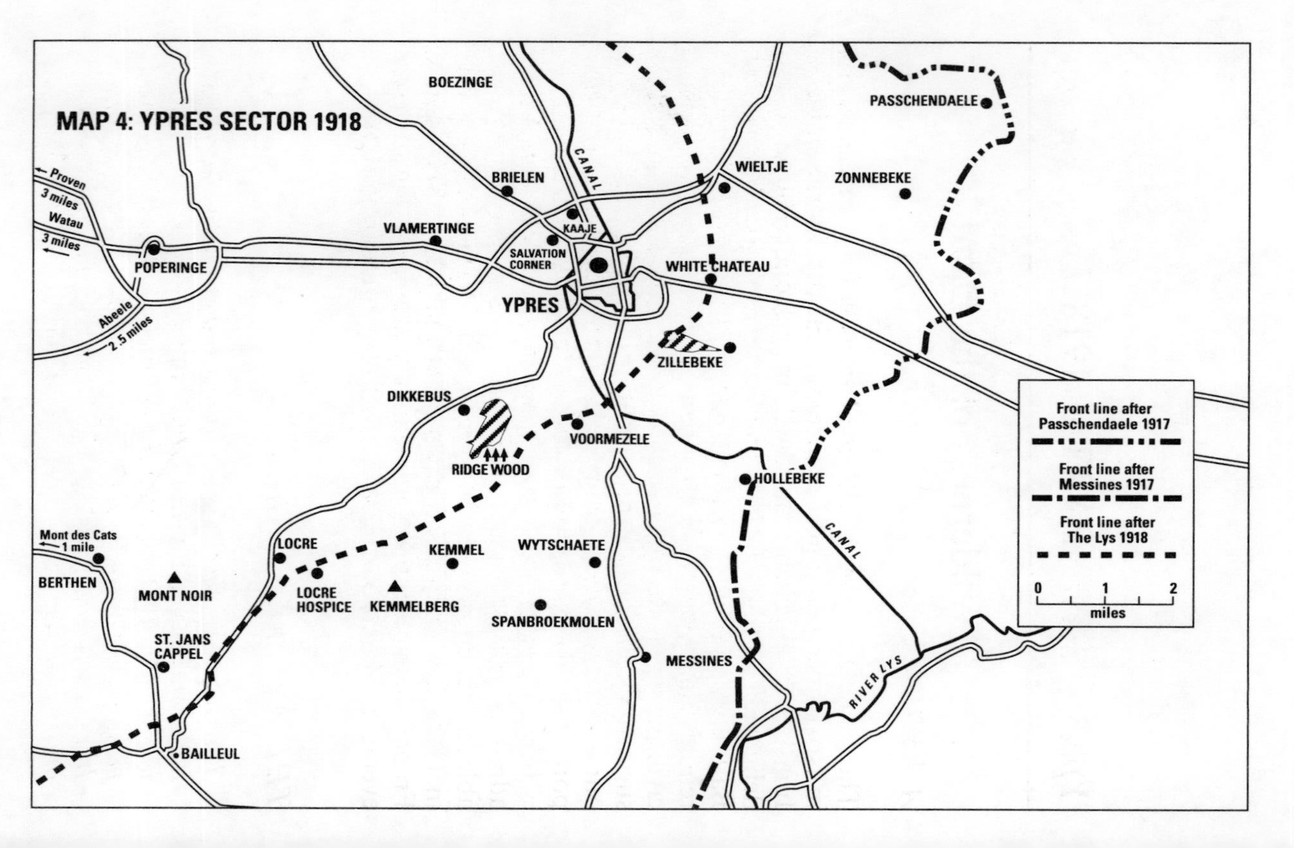

MAP 4: YPRES SECTOR 1918

Ypres – Mont des Cats – The Lys – Victory

A RESPITE

The medical authorities classified me as fit for overseas service in November 1917 and I reported to the 4th Battalion Royal Inniskilling Fusiliers, stationed near Londonderry. I was delighted to find several friends there from the old 8th Battalion, especially my very good pal Bill Ellis, with whom I reminisced at length. We trained hard in the field but led a civilised life with some leisure time. On several occasions survivors from ships torpedoed off Loch Swilly were put up at our camp, the largest group being from the American transport *Tuscania*, consisting of about 1000 officers and men.

In the period I was awaiting my return to Flanders I must admit to finding life most agreeable. During short leaves I was able to spend time with May, mostly in Dublin, once or twice in Tipperary, and to visit my mother and father. My recall to France did not happen immediately, not until the dramatic events in March on the Western Front brought it about.

THE ENEMY STRIKES

The failure of the Russian offensive against the Germans and the subsequent peace terms imposed on the Bolsheviks in February 1918 enabled the Germans to transfer a large part of their army from the Eastern to the Western Front. In the early hours of 21st March the Germans launched a massive attack on the heavily outnumbered British forces over a 50 mile front on either side of St Quentin, south of Arras. By the 5th April they had advanced between 30 and 40 miles, unprecedented on the Western Front. The 16th Division, which included the 7/8th Inniskilling Fusiliers, was one of the many that bore the full brunt of the attack and suffered severe casualties.

Every available man was now needed. For the third time I prepared to set off for France, but under circumstances very different from before. My letter of recall read:

The General Officer Commander-in-Chief

War Office
9th April 1918

Lieut. M.P.L. Cooper

I am directed to request that you will order the above named officer to join the British Armies in France.

He should report personally to the Embarkation Commandant, Southampton, before 3.0 p.m. on the 20th inst, and if passing through London, travel by the train leaving Waterloo Station at 11.35 a.m. on that date.

The officer should be advised to provide his own food, as there is seldom time to obtain any after his arrival at Southampton, before embarking, and no meals are obtainable on the ships.

Military Secretary

Gloom prevailed as we read Haig's order of the day stating that our army was fighting with its 'back to the wall'. On 16th April I said goodbye; May was expecting a baby in a matter of days. I spent the night in London with my sister Carrie and her husband, left Waterloo the next day for Southampton and crossed over to Le Havre. As I sailed in the mail boat I thought of the first occasion my division had embarked, inspired with enthusiasm and hope. Now, two years later, that same 16th Division had completed its task, had become extinct as a fighting force, the price of its heroic defence against General Ludendorff's overwhelming onslaught against the British Army. We were now fighting a desperate rearguard action to stop this massive offensive from reaching the Channel Ports.

AN UNEASY TRAIN JOURNEY

I reported to the base camp at Harfleur in Normandy where I spent several days, finding time even to dine at 'Tortonis'. I was now to join the 1st Inniskilling Fusiliers. I left Le Havre by train at midnight, arriving at Rouen in the morning, where I had breakfast and lunch. I was able to see something of the city and was reminded of when I came here from Loos two years ago to the Military Hospital. I returned to the station where I joined a large draft of men with two officers. The carriage had broken windows, no corridors, no lights, and knowing that troop trains usually went slowly and were likely to stop for long periods we ensured we had a supply of candles. The men, as so often the case, had to travel in rail-trucks. Just before we pulled out of the station the Railway Transport Officer told me I was the senior officer on the train, the implications of which were soon to be brought home to me.

After dark we took off our puttees and boots and settled down for the night. Two of us laid our valises, or 'fleabags', on the seats, the third used the floor. The train jogged along slowly, halting frequently in sidings, until nearly midnight, when we were awakened by a loud crash. The train had stopped, it was dark, and further explosions followed. Peering out of the window I saw we were at a station and could just make out the name 'Amiens'.

Large shells were bursting on each side of the track and close to the station, while at the same time one of our own guns nearby was firing. I knew from reports that the Germans must by now be only a few miles from Amiens and that improvised units made up of orderlies, signallers, batmen and others had been rushed in to try and fill the gaps and hold the attack. It occurred to me that the enemy might at that moment be advancing on the town, which was at the junction of the British and French armies. Being the senior officer on the train and responsible for all the soldiers on board I felt most uncomfortable and somewhat inadequate at that moment, especially without boots and puttees!

I had visions of the enemy driving into the town with the only British force immediately available shut away in trucks, caught with their boots off, their officers not even knowing where the nearest supply of ammunition could be found. There followed an anxious moment during which I felt let down by the Transport Officer at Rouen for not giving me more information, and annoyed with myself for not asking.

We scrambled into our boots in the dark, thinking it wiser not to light the candles. The shelling continued. Fortunately I waited a few minutes, and what a long few minutes they were. The train then gave a sudden lurch, groaned, began twisting its way through a network of lines pitted with shell craters, and slowly drew away from the station and the bursting shells. We had been there for only 5 minutes but they had been some of the most anxious I can remember. Soon we were continuing our journey, no longer heading towards the front but moving northwards.

The Germans were now much stronger as a result of transferring their army from the defunct Russian front. All along the route we could see evidence of their activity; Bethune was nearly in ruins, Hazebrouck badly battered, the railway line damaged in many places.

It was nightfall when the train stopped north of St Omer. We marched to the camp at Millam, about 35 miles behind the front. A large draft of officers and men had already collected there to reinforce the 36th Ulster Division. The sky to the east was bright with flame and we could hear the continuous and intense thunder of distant guns, and feel the hut itself vibrate. Even those of us who had been in the line before had never heard anything like it, we wondered how anyone could live in such an inferno.

On 9th April, at the time the War Office letter recalling Matthew to France was on its way, the Germans launched a second major offensive, the Battle of the Lys. They struck about 10 miles south of Messines – Matthew's old battleground. The enemy advanced 10 miles through an Allied defence line which had been weakened by troop withdrawals to meet the main German thrust on the 21st March in the St Quentin sector. The British defence in the Lys area also held but only after desperate and heroic fighting, which included resistance by divisions that were 'resting' after withdrawal from the St Quentin battle. It meant giving up much of the land gained at Passchendaele at such terrible cost the previous year to prevent the now enlarged Ypres Salient from being outflanked and to release more troops to check this latest German advance. At this point in the war, for the first time, the British Army was near to exhaustion.

Stopped from driving westwards beyond the Lys, the enemy changed its thrust northwards and threatened the British positions on Kemmel Hill, the Messines Ridge and what was now left of the Ypres Salient. The Messines Ridge was evacuated, the town of Bailleul fell, followed by Wytschaete. Enemy assaults on Kemmel Hill were at first repulsed.

French reinforcements were sent and took over the defence of the Kemmel sector, but the vantage point of Kemmel Hill fell to the Germans on 25th April, a bitter blow after so many years. The Battle of the Lys was then brought to an end and the line stabilised, but attacks continued on the small perimeter still left around Ypres.

During his journey back to the front Matthew would probably not have been aware of the full extent of the ground lost, particularly in and around Messines and Kemmel Hill, which later he would be shocked to see for himself.

RETURNING TO YPRES

I met a few old friends during the few days I was at Millam and as there was nothing much to do we used to visit St Omer and walk the three miles to Watten in the evening for dinner. It was better than sitting in a shell hole full of water being straffed by the Boche. I was sorry when two of my friends, Reggie Heard and Spurgeon, left ahead of me to join the 9th Battalion. Soon afterwards I received my orders, that I was to leave the following morning and join the 1st Battalion in the line at Ypres. All the time we could hear the terrific bombardment, making the prospect of going up to the front hardly a cheery one. I longed to hear from May and prayed to God for courage and strength, that He might comfort my darling wife and bring me back again to her. How strange to think I was probably a father, but didn't know it.

About twenty of us left the camp on foot at 3 o'clock in the morning. The gunfire from the general direction of Kemmel had reached such intensity that even at that distance the ground around us shook and the air pulsated. It was daybreak by the time we had covered the five miles to Bollezeele, where we entrained in goods-trucks and travelled for several hours towards the line, listening all the time to the bombardment, which by now had become stunning. As we travelled I wondered at the strange mystery of this war, men under these conditions in good spirits, British soldiers singing while they marched and indulging in comic exchanges.

We got out of the train at Poperinge and continued our journey on foot. We passed long lines of Belgian civilians crowding the roads, hurrying away from the battle, carrying their possessions in handcarts and parcels. Infantry battalions and gun batteries were also moving back, the significance of which we found depressing as we continued our way forward. The town was almost deserted, being shelled by large calibre guns, three or four rounds falling every minute, causing havoc to the buildings. A shell hit a house as we were passing it, tearing a large gap and blowing much of the stonework and its fragments over our heads. We succeeded in finding our new battalion's transport lines outside Poperinge, where I had lunch, shaved, and best of all, found three letters from May. We heard that the Germans were making yet another effort to take Ypres. The Quartermaster did not sound optimistic, telling us over a bully-beef lunch that the battle was still undecided. The general opinion was that the rest of the Salient would be lost, including the ancient town itself, which had held out so valiantly for nearly four years. We felt that going up to the front would turn out to be a forlorn venture.

My instructions were to go up to the canal bank in Ypres and join the 1st Battalion in the line. Taking to the road again we passed through the ruins of Vlamertinge, which was under heavy shell-fire. The battle was raging on all sides. It was a stirring sight to see batteries of guns in action, stretched in a long line, sweat dripping from the gun teams, stripped to the waist. At last we approached the outskirts of Ypres, turned the bend at 'Salvation Corner' and went on towards the canal bank. The road was still being shelled as we marched. The man beside me was hit in the jaw but fortunately we were beside a Casualty Clearing Station and were able to take him in.

Ypres, the place which had witnessed the hottest fighting in the war, was a mass of ruins and blasted trees, a scene of indescribable desolation. Here was testimony to the brutal lust of Germany for imperial domination which brought us into the war. It was also the monument to the many thousands of brave men who had already given their all to secure a world that would be a decent place for others to live in.

BELEAGURED YPRES

It was just before dark on the 29th April when we reached the dugouts on the canal bank and joined the 1st Battalion. That day the Germans had made a supreme effort to take Ypres, the bastion which still defied them and protected the left of our battle line. So short was the distance to the sea that if the enemy should succeed in taking the town it would imperil our whole position in Flanders and force on us a costly retreat. We were told there had been no let-up in the attack throughout the day. Our defence had stood firm.

That first night we were in the reserve line, about a mile behind the front, in a comfortable dugout, one of many which honeycombed the canal bank. For the next few days the shelling was pretty hot and I found myself again in the once familiar role of taking up a wiring party. At dawn we 'stood-to', manning the trenches on the top of the bank. That was the worst part of the day as we would be shelled for about an hour and always expected an attack to follow such an intense bombardment. The dugouts did not give us complete protection from enemy shelling, as we discovered when a large shell fell outside the one next to ours housing the mess staff and batmen. We rushed out and found our cook had been hit although inside the dugout at the time. He died shortly afterwards.

We worked all day, usually in view of the enemy, putting up wire entanglements in front of our position and repairing the damage done by the morning's shelling. But we were always cheerful around the mess-table at night, in large measure due to Sammy Butler, a wit of no small talent, who possessed a sense of humour that brightened many a dark moment. On 2nd May I received a wire from May's nursing home, sent three days before, saying: 'Boy Both Splendid'; what wonderful news. I have a son now but I am not sure if he is going to have a father. For the next few days I had no more letters and wondered how my darling girlie was getting on.

By now the British High Command had decided against evacuating Ypres, a withdrawal having previously been very much on the cards. The Sappers standing by to blow the bridges had been ordered to return to their units, any movement of guns to the rear had been halted. Poor old Ypres, smoking and battered, had survived.

The Belgians continue to this day to recognise the immense sacrifice made by British and Commonwealth soldiers in resisting the fierce attacks mounted by the Germans against Ypres over four years. Every evening at 8 pm the population of Ypres still pay homage to our soldiers who lost their lives in that heroic defence; traffic is halted while Belgian buglers form up on the road in front of the Menin Gate memorial in the town and sound the Last Post.

CONFINED TO A PILL-BOX

A week later I took my platoon up to the front line at Wieltje, about two miles on the far side of Ypres. The ground was water-logged making it impossible to dig trenches. We were in old German concrete pill-boxes dating back to when they held the position, which meant they faced the wrong way for us, the entrance being in full view of the enemy. There were a lot of these emplacements, some smaller than any I had ever seen before. We occupied four of them, separated by as little as 20 yards. They had two tiny compartments inside, barely 5 × 4 × 4 feet, in which it was usual for four of us to crouch.

By day we dare not move and had to lie doggo inside, sitting with our knees up in that cramped space for as long as 15 hours; my Platoon Sergeant, two men and myself in one of them. It required continual vigilance on our part to prevent the Boche from surprising us at night and capturing our posts. It was not so dangerous after dark to walk about in the open so I decided on a system of continuous night patrols. I gave orders that if the enemy appeared the patrol was to give the alarm and make for the nearest pill-box and join in the defence of the position. This meant negotiating battlefield debris in the dark, stumbling into shell holes, always taking care not to bump accidentally into an enemy outpost. In this way we were able to keep watch over the immediate vicinity after dusk.

Each day we 'stood-to' shortly before dawn and 'stood-down' at 4.30 am, scrambling back into our shelters. We took turns to sleep during the day, always with one sentry in each post constantly on the look-out. We were ready to defend our position as best we could in the event of an attack. It seemed to us as though we were being shelled all day, although we had been careful not to reveal exactly which blockhouses we were occupying at any one time. The outlook was bleak, especially having to look at a skull protruding from a pool of dirty water just in front of us.

The pill-boxes which the enemy occupied were about 200 yards away but they had the advantage that they were built facing us so they did not have the same problem in concealing their movements by day.

Two incidents occurred early on, the first was in the early hours of one morning when I ordered the troops to stand-to. One of the men in my pill-box, a strong and well-built fellow, wearing the ribbon of the Military Medal which he won on the Somme, refused to come out and stayed inside reclining and grinning. This was a situation an officer dreaded, all the more in the face of an enemy only yards away. I went over to him and repeated the order; still with no result. I drew my revolver, looked at him straight in the eye, repeated the order and waited. He pondered for a moment, then, mercifully, he stood up and said 'If that's the way you feel about it, I'll come out', and he did, joining the other men behind a few sandbags in front of the pill-box. It was a relief to me, I cannot tell how I would have reacted had he again refused. I knew that other officers had also been involved in incidents with this man.

The other episode involved the second-in-command, who did not approve of my relying for defence on continuous patrolling at night and thought I should seal off each pill-box with barbed wire. As it happened, I had previously agreed my plan with Captain May, my Company Commander. However he reported me to the Colonel, saying I was 'a young officer who was not concerned with the safety of his men'. As I heard no more about it I assumed that Captain May had backed me. I had the last laugh too, not long afterwards he lost his rank on ceasing to be second-in-command and reverted to Lieutenant, at the very time I was promoted to acting Captain!

Our Company Commander came up to see us each night. His visits were a tonic as he was an unfailing optimist and brought us letters from home. I still had heard nothing from home since the telegram and wondered how my darling May was getting on after the birth of my son over a week ago.

Enemy shelling continued all around our posts and as this wierd life continued I found consolation in the verse from the hymn 'Lead, Kindly Light':

'*So long Thy power hath blest me, sure it still*
Will lead me on,
O'er moor and fen, o'er crag and torrent, till
The night is gone;'

BACK IN SUPPORT

After five days we were told we would be leaving these front line concrete shelters to return to the comparative peace of the canal bank. My instructions were that when relieved by another platoon I was to follow the light railway line to the canal. When the time came we were all very tired, it was pitch dark, hardly any Very lights were being fired. I found the rail track and led my men along it only to realise after a few moments that I was moving towards the German lines. I turned my party around in some haste.

A little later I was leading my platoon in single file along the railway track at the place where it spanned the canal on a construction of timber columns and beams. I managed to fall between the sleepers at a place where some of the cross-beams were missing. Fortunately I instinctively grabbed the rails on each side as I fell and saved myself from a nasty drop on to jagged rocks sticking up from the canal bed below. Now fully awakened I passed a warning to the others coming along behind!

We were glad to be back at the canal bank as the Germans were now keeping fairly quiet and for a short time we could get some peace. It was a relief to get away from those cramped, dark little pill-boxes and to be able to walk about in daylight. I took the company down to the baths, always a popular activity with the troops, who welcomed the prospect of a clean-up. On Sunday we went to a parade church service on the canal bank, simple and comforting. At last some letters arrived from May; she was delighted with the baby. The poor little girl had been through a bad time but was getting better now and told me all sorts of wonderful things about our little son, making me wonder when I would see him. I also heard that my friend Reggie was wounded, a nice one, in the arm.

The Company Commander had gone for a rest and I took over from him. The next night we were due back in the support line and I mustered the company and marched them to Kaaje, close to Ypres. Our spirits fell somewhat when we heard heavy shelling at 'Dead End', which lay in our path about ten minutes away. We filed along the canal bank, past the cemetery towards the bridge at Ypres, a well known danger spot, where on our arrival the shelling abruptly stopped. We thanked Providence, crossed the bridge quickly in sections, and made our way over a patch of badly churned up ground where a large artillery wagon lay on its side with its dead driver. Further up the road when we were nearing our position we passed a ruined house on which was written 'Abandon hope all ye who pass by here', but I don't think we did, whatever we may have felt.

That night I shared a cellar with Sammy Butler in a ruined house. We described to each other from our imagination the joy of walking again down the main street of our home towns. This somehow served to highlight the enormity of the contrast between that and the life we were now experiencing. Ye gods what a difference! When we woke up he found his voice had gone, my eyes were paining and I had white blisters on my eyeballs, both of us were on the point of vomiting. The enemy was firing mustard gas. My eyes were sore for some time and took several weeks to recover.

It was a relief during the period we were in support when morning came, enemy straffing would be suspended for a time and the threat of an attack had diminished. The spring weather was lovely and from our position we could watch the dust flying from the great ruins of Ypres about a mile away. It was being constantly shelled, but the ever defiant, dignified and jagged finger of the Cloth Hall remained pointing to the sky. It was described in the newspaper as 'the glorious ruins of that ancient Flemish city'. As enemy shelling by day was only slight we could view this battered region, listen to the drone of aeroplane engines overhead and try to appreciate the warm and sunny weather we were having.

I was very happy to get six letters from my darling and one from my dear friend Bill Ellis. One night, shortly before stand-to, I thought of the line from the ever popular war song:

'Though your lads are far away, they dream of Home'.

AT ALL COSTS

The next day I took the company up to the front line, spacing out three of my platoons in outpost trenches on the fringe of a wood, each with an officer. I set up my headquarters in a dugout excavated under the ruins of the famous 'White Chateau', close to 'Hell Fire Corner', the mansion which featured so prominently in the early months of the war, at the First Battle of Ypres. We went to ground by day living by candlelight, working by night on improving our defences. Each dawn we awaited an attack, knowing that if it came there would be no retreat, every man was expected to die at his post.

One night we were told an attack was imminent and the line was to be held at all costs, given further emphasis by the warning that in the event of an attack our artillery barrage and machine-gun fire would be put down behind our position! I joined my small group comprising my Sergeant-Major, Signallers and Lewis Gun Team, ensuring we were armed with all the bombs and ammunition we might need. I had done all I could and there was nothing more now but to wait. I thought with wry amusement of the advice given us from above that the safest place for us could well be in the forward enemy trenches as we would then avoid their preliminary barrage! I pictured my company interspersed among German storm-troopers who were lined up ready to attack. I also remembered an earlier formal publication to young officers seeking to arouse their spirit of aggression, whose title, *Am I As Offensive As I Might Be*?, caused much raucous laughter.

We waited through that long night, witnessing at one period a savage bombardment on our troops to the right, but no attack came. We heard later that the Germans had unexpectedly changed their plan and had started to move their units in front of us to the south. The next morning I made my rounds and was held up for about a quarter of an hour, sitting on a duckboard, while all round fell a succession of 'whizz-bangs' – high velocity light shells whose burst is heard before the sound of the gun.

MY PILL-BOX FRIEND AGAIN

On 22nd May we went back to Brielen, to a collection of derelict huts and shelters, where we were able again to get used to daylight, had a chance to clean up and to make up for lost sleep. We were heartened to hear that the French had made a successful attack in the region of Dikkebus. On arrival I found eight letters from May. We were able to relax during this period and I took the opportunity to visit Dunkirk.

I had another incident with the man who refused to get out of the pill-box that morning at Wieltje. I was holding a pay parade sitting in a small sandbagged shelter, the Quarter-master Sergeant alongside me with the pay-rolls calling out each man's name in turn and the sum he was to receive. The Company Sergeant-Major stood between the entrance to the shelter and my table, repeating the name to the men clustered outside. Eventually the name of my friend was reached. The amount specified was 'five francs' – the minimum anyone could be paid no matter how many 'stoppages' he had incurred as punishment for offences. He came in, saluted and stood before me, beside the Sergeant-Major. I handed him five francs. He picked them up, threw them back on the table with disgust, and said 'That's no use to me'. The Sergeant-Major laid his hand on the man's shoulder, whereupon the soldier hit him under the chin, knocking him stone-cold to the floor. The two junior NCO's standing near the door backed away as the man turned and faced them. I stood up, went to the entrance, ordered an NCO and several men standing outside to place the man under arrest and take him to the guardroom. My friend gave the same sort of laugh he gave at the pill-box, saying disarmingly 'You needn't worry, I'll go quietly'; and he did.

Our spell in reserve was over and we returned to the support line. Three of us, the Company Commander, Sammy and I, were at Wilson's Farm living in a wooden hut with a tin roof. We hoped the enemy would pay us no attention as the protection offered by the construction was only capable, we agreed, of keeping off the rain. The enemy must have thought these huts were unoccupied so we did nothing to cause him to think otherwise, ignoring any stray shells that came our way. We spent the night reinforcing the defences of the support line, digging trenches and putting up wire, returning to the hut by day.

We wondered if the war would ever end; we had had too much of it. The day was aggravated for me by troublesome teeth which I hoped I would be able to have seen to in ten days or so. I made a note of our activities one day, which read:

28th May 1918

Dawn:	Stand-to
3.45 am:	Breakfast
until 2 pm:	Slept and rested
2-3 pm:	Scathing criticism of all instigators of war
3 pm:	Lunch
3.30-5 pm:	Played cards, 'Slippery Sam'
5 pm:	Tea and rude remarks about our artillery
9 pm:	Dinner; denounced multilation of this wretched country. Spirits not high.
10 pm:	Stand-to. Hopeless sunset
after sunset:	Stand-down
until dawn:	Visited sentry posts

'NAPOO'

On the 1st June I took out a night patrol of 12 men, larger than usual, on a 3-hour reconnaissance, to find out if two farms were occupied by the enemy and if possible, which German unit was in them. The ground we now inhabited had been fought over backwards and forwards for almost four years. It was a swamp of mud, covered in shell holes, the line of the trench no longer defined as in other parts of the battle line. The enemy kept shifting his position, as we did, and we had to know exactly where he was.

My patrol advanced down a light railway track which was raised above the mud, with two men leading, two on each flank, and two protecting the rear. I was leading the centre group and ensured that only two men moved forward at any one time. After proceeding carefully in this way we came across two British rifles abandoned by some ill-fated patrol which must have been performing a similar task. It was shortly before dawn when we neared an enemy post, where the enemy seemed nervous and regularly sent up Very lights. There was no reasonable chance of taking a prisoner but I was able to pin-point their position, which was not at either of the two suspected locations.

On our return we were told that a large-scale German attack was probable at dawn. In that case our breakfast would be 'napoo', the British soldier's attempt at French, slang for 'done for'. On leaving our dugouts that night we shook hands and went to our platoons to await the deluge of shells which would herald the attack. Instead, our artillery put down a heavy bombardment during the hours around daybreak. It was well into the morning but still no attack came, perhaps our shelling had restrained them. On our return to the dugout Sammy and I drank 'Damnation to the Kaiser' and fell asleep.

FEELS LIKE PEACETIME

We were told that our Belgian allies were to take over our sector of the line on 4th June. The day before we were due to be relieved several of their officers arrived to make preparations. In a mixture of bad French on our part, and equally bad English on theirs, we told them what we considered the important points about the front they would be holding. They had been trained in England and were about to undergo their first experience in the line. How we admired their new uniforms, swords and kid gloves, and thought they must be feeling as we did on first taking over a part of the line.

The following day when the change-over was completed we were informed, yet again, there would be an attack that night. As Sammy and I said goodbye to our Belgian friends on leaving the dugout to start on our way back we found ourselves looking over our shoulders anxiously, hoping we would not see the expected attack materialise before the Belgians had had time to accustom themselves to their new line.

We were now due for a rest period and during the night we marched to the junction of the light railway at No. 4 Bridge on the canal bank. Here our brigade was entrained in small open trucks, and though cold and uncomfortable, we were all cheerful at leaving the line behind. As dawn came it was a delight to find we were passing sleepy farmhouses and fields of waving green crops. No Greek warrior of old returning from the wars could have revelled more joyously in seeing again his native land than we did in those scenes of peaceful countryside and orderly cultivation.

It was 5 am when we reached 'Tunnellers Camp' near Proven, a few miles from Poperinge, where we stayed for several days. We then continued our journey by train until we arrived at Rubrouck, north of St Omer, about 20 miles behind the line. I found myself in the same billet I had occupied a year before, but then I was with my dear old pals Robbins and Carrothers, both now dead, and Charlesworth a prisoner.

The name of 2/Lieut J.S. Carrothers is inscribed on the memorial wall at Tyne Cot Military Cemetery near Passchendaele in the long roll of the Royal Inniskilling Fusiliers who, with those from so many other gallant regiments, fell in the Ypres Salient and have no known grave. During the assault on the Messinges Ridge he had commanded the party, alongside Matthew's, going back and forth across the battlefield, carrying over 1000 shells into Wytschate.

On the same occasion, 2/Lieut A.H. Robbins had commanded the platoon which carried 100 boxes of small arms ammunition for the Machine Gun Company over a distance of two miles, in relays, over a period of 17 hours.

On returning to Proven I found a letter from my sister Carrie saying that my dear brother Austin, serving with a Machine Gun Company, had been reported missing. I prayed that he would turn up or had been taken prisoner. Another letter, from my good friend Bill Ellis, told me that poor Jumbo Hornby had died of his wounds. He was one of the best, had commanded the second wave of the large-scale raid on the Messines Ridge in June 1917 in which I had taken part. We had sent out a search party for him when he did not return, who found him, badly wounded, and brought him back to our lines, from where he was taken home to England. We were told of his award of the Military Cross shortly after the raid.

We now found ourselves able to live a life which must have resembled peacetime soldiering, with morning parades, training, games in the afternoon and some form of amusement in the evening. One difference was that on several nights enemy aeroplanes flew overhead and dropped bombs, but they mostly fell in a field alongside and being accustomed to bombardment at night some of us did not even wake up. On a day-off I took a lorry to Dunkirk and walked around the town. Several times I rode with one or two friends to call at an excellent restaurant nearby where we would have lunch or dinner, served by a one-time butler of the local chateau, who must have had access to the family cellar and its pink sparkling Bergundy!

It was now the middle of June and we had a number of alerts warning us of an imminent enemy attack. On most days now we used to leave the camp at dawn and travel by light railway to Poperinge to dig trenches for what was called the

Blue Line, returning shortly after midday. The Blue Line was a defence behind the British front whose construction was prompted by the German breakthrough in March. In addition to soldiers we used Chinese labourers, all of us digging miles of defences, almost as far as the sea. During this period we also continued our training and carried out practice attacks, including one on the Blue Line itself.

As we were still out of the front line we had some leisure time and I was able to go riding with two friends, have a day at a horse show in Proven, visit the nearby town of Wormhout with two friends, and watch a football match between a Belgian regiment and ourselves – ending happily in a draw. During a Sports Day, in which our battalion took part, I met someone who had known my brother Austin, but he had no information about what had happened to him.

ALAS MESSINES!

Rumours were again spreading of a coming German attack and I was not surprised when at the beginning of July we were ordered back to the front, this time to relieve the French in the area of Mont des Cats. When we got there we found every farmhouse had been destroyed by shell-fire, the occupants having left their homes in a hurry without taking their crops or vegetables with them.

The hill was an exceptional vantage point and from the top we had a panoramic view of the whole area and could see our own and the enemy front lines a few miles ahead. In the distance lay the Messines Ridge, the ground we had captured at the cost of so much blood, so many lives, which was now again in enemy hands. The German onslaught across the River Lys in April had recaptured all our gains at the victorious Battle of Messines the previous year and forced the evacuation of the ground taken later, at such sacrifice, at Passchendaele. Kemmel Hill, our one-time beacon, was now battered out of recognition, reduced to a few stark, branchless trees; not a blade of grass, not a touch of green. Areas that we knew as comparatively peaceful were now bespattered with shell holes. Locre was in ruins, the Hospice of happy memories where the Nuns had so graciously served us many appetising meals had been levelled to the ground and was now the scene of bitter fighting.

The town of Bailleul, where I had arrived by train with my old 8th Battalion nearly two years before on first coming to Kemmel from Loos, was also in enemy hands, but at least the enemy was paying dearly for its possession as our guns bombarded it, causing it to erupt with brick dust and smoke. It was a bitter pill to swallow and as I looked at it all and thought back I found it difficult to imagine how victory could ever be ours.

While in reserve we lived in a pleasant little hut made of wood and corrugated iron, open to the air. At night we marched up to the line through the ruined village of Berthen to the edge of Mont Noir where we helped to dig trenches. We were invariably shelled while working there so we hailed the approach of dawn when we were able to set off on the five mile march back to our own position.

WELCOME DIVERSIONS

At that time it was customary for about a tenth of the battalion to be at a rest camp at Bonningues, about 10 miles west of St Omer. My turn now came for a few days at the camp and while there I at last had the opportunity to go to the dentist, at Houlle, where I was kept overnight at the hospital. An air raid took place during the night and being used to the protection of a trench or dugout my friend and I felt very vulnerable. We strove to overcome an urge to get under the bed when bombs whistled through the air and exploded around the building. Unfortunately there were a number of shell-shock patients in the hospital who could not be restrained by the doctors and nurses and rushed from their beds in their night clothes, shrieking as they ran to a nearby wood.

The next day I returned to the rest camp and then back to

the line, where I found more letters and had the good news that my brother Austin was reported safe as a prisoner. I was able to look back on a pleasant little stay at Bonningues.

The German initiative on the Western Front in 1918 came to an end in July. The British attacked at Amiens on 8th August, General Ludendorff's 'black day' for the German Army, followed by the successful Battle of Arras at the end of the month. These victories, together with French successes, paved the way for the great Allied advance.

Early in August I was sent on a course to the Xth Corps Infantry School. I worked hard and very much enjoyed the change, glad at the chance of being able to play hockey almost every day, and to my surprise, receiving an award for bayonet fighting. It was the custom for one officer to stay on for an extra course as an instructor and I was nominated for this.

In the intervening week I went as Liaison Officer to a Canadian squadron of the Flying Corps at Abeele, near Poperinge, where I had my first ever flight. On the last day I persuaded the Commanding Officer to let me go up a second time and we flew over Ypres, then on to Lens, the two battle areas where I had spent so much of my time. Below us stretched the vast countryside, looking like a sand-model, the towns appearing as though built of children's bricks. Several enemy 'archies' burst near us but it was the sudden appearance of an enemy plane that hastened our return to base; our plane was unarmed!

I completed the second course in mid-October and reported to 36th Reception Camp at Roesbrugge, a few miles north of Poperinge. I found it a bit lonely at the camp, no letters, away from my friends in the battalion, nothing much to do, but it afforded the great luxury of sleeping in a bed. I received an unexpected surprise when I was told that I would soon be due for home leave, although this time I had only been back in France for six months. I doubted if I would in fact be given leave just yet and expected to return first to the front for a further spell. That was what happened, but I had no complaints as I had been having a good time at the school while many others were facing death.

THE HOUR BEFORE DAWN

During the period I had been out of the line the tide of war had turned. In March General Foch had been appointed Generalissimo of the Allied Armies and one hand was now on the helm. The tremendous German onslaught launched in March had been brought to a standstill and our troops were sweeping forward in a series of victories. The Ypres Salient, so long the symbol of our resolve, was now far behind our line and we were driving the enemy over the River Lys beyond the old Messines battlefield.

A few days later the camp moved from Roesbrugge to a location beyond Poperinge and I set off on horseback with my friend Howard to join them, calling in on the way at the well-known restaurant, 'Skindles' - Poperinge's reminder of Maidenhead. Old 'Pops' still looked itself despite having more of its houses wrecked. We left our horses at Poperinge and continued on foot, searching around the area for the camp, but could not find it. The battle had swept so swiftly through and beyond the Salient that there was as yet little organisation behind the line. It was dark and we were tired.

The pre-war inhabitants of this area had gone a long time ago, leaving only the flash and thunder of war, but these could not disturb the many thousands who now slept in this ground. They, the vanished army, had sown the seed and it now fell to those who had survived to sweep forward and reap the harvest. In that inky darkness, amid an appalling silence, we wandered in that wilderness of the dead. It was like the darkest hour before the dawn.

At last we saw a light. It turned out to be a field hospital near Brielen, where we were given dinner, bed and breakfast. We set off in the morning, again on foot, and after three hours came across the camp. My orders were to return to my battalion at the front, now a long way ahead as it swept forward with the rapid advance of the Allies.

The next day we went in a rail truck from Vlamertinge to Ledegem, five miles north of Menin. The first stop on the way was Ypres station, which had not been used for years and where the buildings were rubble. We passed slowly over the great four-year battlefield, never before having seen any place which had suffered so much devastation. There was no grass or greenery, all that remained of Houthulst Forest were short jagged stumps. There were derelict tanks, crashed aeroplanes, an abundance of destroyed guns, broken rifles and abandoned equipment. Many dead were as yet unburied, and everywhere there lingered that smell of decomposition and gas which was always associated with Ypres.

The great expanse of the one-time Salient and the devastated country on both sides of the line were deserted. Our route took us over Passchendaele, the scene of such fearful fighting a year ago. As we continued several miles further the desolation gradually gave way to cultivation. The rail cattle-truck was crowded and we were stiff by the time we reached Ledegem. I searched for two hours on foot before finding a billet for the night, in a farmhouse which had been stripped of almost everything by the Germans before they fled. In the morning I jumped lorries to Harelbeke, just north of Courtrai, which had been given up by the enemy a week before. The inhabitants were worn and thin but looked happy and gave us an enthusiastic welcome. Everywhere flags were flying.

LAST TIME AT THE FRONT

The enemy were being driven back so quickly it was difficult to find my unit. I eventually traced our quartermaster stores to a little farm. As I rode towards the front from the transport lines I ran into some shelling on the road, and on each side I saw large German guns which had been abandoned. I found the battalion holding a line of isolated farmhouses, largely intact, in which the owners still lived. Enemy rearguards were putting up stout resistance supported by machine-guns and artillery but were being mopped up as we pushed on.

We were now engaged in open warfare. The days of the trenches were over, the enemy had been chased from his burrows. The decisive stage of the long conflict had been reached. We attacked almost every day and advanced further against an enemy that was now relying on concealed machine-gun nests to hold up our advance. The opposing lines were much further apart than they were during the period of static warfare but it was unwise to sit near a window that faced the enemy, there were still plenty of bullets flying about.

A few days later I left the front, going on ahead to arrange billets in the nearby village of Hulste, just north of Courtrai. I had a premonition that this would be my last sight of the battle zone, which hastened my departure, spurred on admittedly by the enemy's desultory shell-fire. I left the line at dawn on a bicycle, pedalling over roads broken by shell-holes. I called at farmhouses in the billeting area, spoke to the owners, allotted houses, stables and barns to platoons, sections and headquarters. Each company had a representative with me to act as guide and together we chalked up unit names on the doors and drew rough sketches. The battalion arrived shortly after 3 am and were in their billets by 5 am. Reveille was set for 8 am with a two mile march to Lendelede for baths, and back for breakfast.

The next day was a memorable one for the battalion, we marched through the town of Courtrai, drums and fifes leading, to a thunderous reception from the inhabitants, most of whom were wearing clogs on their bare feet. I led C Company, which I now commanded, on what was an emotional and unforgettable occasion.

VICTORY

A few days later I was granted 10 days furlough and set off for home with a loaded pack and greatcoat. The railway system had not caught up with us so I adopted the usual mode of travel, jumping motor lorries, and reached Menin after a series of short rides. The town had been in German hands during the war and was now deserted and badly damaged. I spent the night in the chateau with a few others who were going on leave. The Kaiser used to stay there when visiting this part of the front, but it would have been different then, the interior now being empty and bare, stripped by the Germans before they left.

We got a train from Menin, taking some satisfaction in finding the station had been almost completely destroyed by the striking power of our airmen – a sentiment that may not have been shared by our Belgian allies! The German retreat was being reported daily and everyone I met on the way and in the Officers' Club in Calais was full of optimism, confident that the war was won. These great days had followed so closely on the darkest. I went on board and it seemed no time before we were approaching the White Cliffs. I felt full of joy at the thought of being back with my family so soon.

The next day I was with May and my baby son, who could so easily have been born without a father. Everywhere there was a feeling of high expectation. My leave was nearly over when my mother rushed into the room with the wonderful news. It was 'Peace'?!

The conflict which had started four years before as a crusade had at last ended in triumph. We had lived to share in this glorious hour of our country. But there were others, our good friends, whom we will never forget, who had given everything and whose last resting places lie along that vast battlefront. From Ypres to St Quentin their graves are a lasting testimony of their fidelity to the cause. To us, their comrades, their memory will ever be fresh. We remember them as they were in the Salient, at Messines and on other battlefields. We will change with time, but we shall always see them as those young merry faces gleaming through the candles in the dugout or again with that look of tense determination when duty demanded sacrifice.

> Their bodies are buried in peace;
> but their names liveth for evermore
>
> [Eccles. 44. 4]

POSTSCRIPT

I did not intend this personal journal to be a history of part of the Great War. It is a collection of personal experiences and feelings as I remember them, put together now, shortly after the Armistice, before memory becomes dimmed by time.

I kept a diary in the trenches during 1918 and have used its day-to-day entries in writing this journal. For 1916 and 1917 I have relied on wartime documents which I retained and on my recollection of many events, personal incidents and emotions which are still fresh in my mind.

It was written for my own satisfaction, to help me to remember those epoch-making, tragic, yet stirring years that made so deep an impression on me and whose influence I shall always feel.

'WE WHO KNEW'

In after years they'll come and see the ground we knew so well;
The road that ran from Kemmel town, the village of Vermelles.
The guide will indicate the place with careless sweep of hand
They'll only see the tombstones and the cultivated land.
But we who knew will see once more that deathless army pass,
And walk with them the vanished trench that lies beneath the grass.
'Tis only we who held it once shall see the line again
And hear the roar of battle rage from Ypres to St Quentin.

Matthew Cooper

Matthew stayed on in the army after the war. He went with his battalion to Upper Silesia in 1921 during the disorder there, then to the British Army of the Rhine, where he wrote this journal. He remained in the army after the war, retiring in 1937, when he became Bursar in a public school in the South of England.

He was recalled from the Reserve in 1939 on the outbreak of war and served on the staff in Southern Command near Salisbury in the rank of Major. During that time his wife May temporarily took on his position at the school. He retired from the army, for the second time, before the end of the war and returned to his job. He took much pleasure in running the local Cadet Company of the Home Guard. Both his sons were regular soldiers and served in the Second World War; the younger is the editor of this journal.

When the war ended he continued as Bursar and with his writing. He and May delighted in good music and between them they organised a local choir of exceptional talent. He was an ardent churchman and became a lay reader. He seldom spoke about his war experiences, but when he did, his reflections were dominated by the spirit of comradeship, unselfishness and humour which made those years endurable, qualities which afterwards he was unable to find, to the extent he had hoped, in contemporary life.

He spent the latter part of his retirement in the village of Garboldisham, Norfolk, where he died in 1969, aged 77. May died in 1990 and is buried in the same churchyard.

[AMC]

ACKNOWLEDGMENTS

The publishers thank the Imperial War Museum for permission to reproduce the following photographs:

Scottish Regiment keeping watch with periscopes
Ruins of Loos
Mine shaft entrance
Slag heap at Philosophe
The road from Kemmel Town
Spanbroekmolen mine crater four days after the explosion
Ulster Division on Messines Ridge
German pillboxes on Messines Ridge
Officers' Mess, Messines Ridge
Royal Inniskilling Fusiliers
Nuns at Major Redmond's grave
German artillery observation balloons
Large Howitzer at 'Salvation Corner'
Bridge over canal, Ypres
'The jagged finger of the Cloth Hall', Ypres
Main Street, Ypres
Locre Hospice

The photograph of Spanbroekmolen crater in 1931 is reproduced by courtesy of TOC H.